"*Battle Ready* is a field manual for the mind. If you desire to think more like Christ, its truths, stories, personal applications and discoveries will undoubtedly lead y[...] peace, hope, and life."

Elisa Morgan, speaker and author

"Relational, emotional, and physical trial[...] miles an hour, making us feel defenseless a[...] powerless. This no longer has to be the case. *Battle Ready*, an exploratory, hands-on book, provides dozens of mind-renewing truths, hope-building exercises, and habit-changing techniques to help you endure the worst of times, with Jesus, as if it was the best of times."

Shannon Ethridge, MA, life/relationship coach and author of 20+ books, including the million-copy bestselling *Every Woman's Battle* series

"Whatever battle you are fighting, Kelly comes alongside and arms you with practical wisdom, biblical truth, and a victorious battle cry, 'Yes, God can!' *Battle Ready* is more than a book; it's a plan to keep at the ready for all life's trials."

Kristin Schell, author of *The Turquoise Table*

"*Battle Ready* is a book that helps proactively prepare us to fight back against doubt, disbelief, and uncertainty in order to live from a stance of determination, resiliency, and faith to be all that God has called us to be. Kelly offers twelve warrior mind-sets, from recognizing the possibilities in working with God to living in humility in order to align our mind with Christ as we proceed into battle from a place of victory. *Battle Ready* provides tangible suggestions of ways to take heart and keep our minds focused on His truth for victorious living."

Dr. Michelle Bengtson, international speaker and author of *Hope Prevails: Insights From a Doctor's Personal Journey through Depression* and the companion *Hope Prevails Bible Study*

"With passion and authenticity, Kelly Balarie delivers a truth-packed feast for the soul in *Battle Ready*. Kelly inspires us to notice our thought patterns so we can change how we think with Scripture as our guide and the Spirit as our strength. Kelly cheers us back to the Daddy of our hearts as we learn the dance of taking each thought captive to Him. This book will wake your heart up to the beauty of God's Word, encourage you to deeply tune in to

God, and grow your affection for your Savior. *Battle Ready* will change minds, hearts, and lives. If you need a transformed mind, let this powerful book, along with the power of Scripture, cheer you on towards the joy and freedom God has for you."

Sarah Beth Marr, author of *Dreaming with God: A Bold Call to Step Out and Follow God's Lead*

"What goes on inside our head often steers us in the wrong direction. We desperately need to do a thought audit to weed out the world's life-sucking lies and replace them with God's life-giving truth. If you're ready to silence the negative voices in your mind, Kelly will lead the way with this powerful book."

Jill Savage, author of *No More Perfect Moms* and *No More Perfect Marriages*

"As I soaked up *Battle Ready*, I was struck by the everyday practicality of its message, as well as the nuggets of gold wisdom in each chapter. Kelly has a special way of vulnerably sharing her own struggles, all while pointing readers to the never-fading truth of Scripture. This book is not just words on a page; it's an invitation to saturate our minds with the wisdom found in God's word. *Battle Ready* will encourage you to see yourself as God's beloved child, and it will inspire you to live boldly—like a warrior ready to follow Christ wherever He leads. You will not only want to read this book but you'll want to mark it to death with a highlighter and pen."

Kendra Broekhuis, author of *Here Goes Nothing: An Introvert's Reckless Attempt to Love Her Neighbor*

"*Battle Ready* is a mental and spiritual boot camp of lessons to prepare you for what life throws at you in the future and heal you from what life threw at you in the past. Kelly's bite-sized pieces of powerful truths make the biblical principles easy to understand and practical to apply. Get ready to wave the flag of victory over the battles you may face."

Sharon Jaynes, author of *Take Hold of the Faith You Long For: Let Go, Move Forward, Live Bold*

"*Battle Ready* is chock-full of reminders, mini-lessons, and truths for every battered and bruised one of us. With honesty and insight, Kelly points to the path where the meek become mighty and the weary wise."

Erin Loechner, blogger at DesignforMankind.com and author of *Chasing Slow*

"Kelly is a prayer warrior who knows firsthand the power and importance of taking captive her thoughts to make them obedient to Christ. If you struggle with negative mental chatter—or a full-blown assault—you'll find *Battle Ready* a practical guide to arresting stray thoughts and making them submissive to Jesus. Whatever your battle, may you grow to have the mind of Christ in you and toward others."

Asheritah Ciuciu, founder of One Thing Alone Ministries and author of *Unwrapping the Names of Jesus: An Advent Devotional* and *Full: Food, Jesus, and the Battle for Satisfaction*

"Kelly has written a powerful, timely, and essential book for our day. There's no fluff here. Well researched and yet so accessible, this book reads like one part manual and one part devotional. Kelly invites us on a journey of transformation that's solidly biblical and profoundly inspirational. It takes time and persistence to change the way we think. Make space in your life and prayerfully work your way through the pages of this book. With God's help you'll discover that you're actually wired for freedom."

Susie Larson, talk radio host, national speaker, and author of *Your Powerful Prayers*

"In a day and age when it's easy to settle for an ordinary existence, Kelly Balarie empowers her readers to choose an extraordinary path toward an extraordinary God. *Battle Ready* invites women to shift thought-patterns, perspectives, and life-purposes in order to become the 'warriors' God created us to be."

Aubrey Sampson, speaker, church planter, and author of *Overcomer: Breaking Down the Walls of Shame and Rebuilding Your Soul* and *Game Changer: Lament and Hope in Seasons of Difficulty*

"In today's culture, it can be all too easy to get stuck in a harmful thought habit that prevents us from being the best version of ourselves. Kelly Balarie's *Battle Ready* is more than just inspiration from a trusted friend. This book is a complete resource that will allow you to reclaim your confidence once and for all. Anyone can bring out their inner warrior using this remarkable guide."

Anne Watson, speaker and author at GodDots.com and host of *The Declare Conference* podcast

"Worry and doubt can plague our minds and threaten to take us down in the toughest of times. *Battle Ready* is an invitation to live differently. We don't have to spend our lives in a constant state of trepidation. Step by step, Kelly points us in a new direction toward a faith-filled life and shows us how to live with deep-seated hope no matter what we face!"

Ruth Schwenk, founder of TheBetterMom.com and author of *The Better Mom* and *Pressing Pause*

"I believe we are living in one of the most profound hours in human history. Out of the ashes God is raising up a generation of warriors by clothing them in His beauty. It is these transformed ones who are destined to transform culture. Mind-sets are foundational to this process. What we believe is who we become. In this book Kelly Balarie presents biblical truth in such a masterful way that it dismantles dysfunctional belief systems and empowers the reader to be 'battle ready' for this journey called life. My prayer is that God would use this book as a catalytic tool in His hands to empower multitudes around the globe."

Darren Davis, senior pastor of The Harbour Church, Fort Lauderdale, Florida

"*Battle Ready* is a training manual for those preparing for a war that is fought and won in the spiritual realm. May I suggest you take a long approach and not rush through your reading. Grab your Bible, journal, and pen and take this step-by-step guide one section, or even one question, at a time. 'Choose decisively,' as Balarie writes, to prepare your mind."

Anna LeBaron, author of *The Polygamist's Daughter*

"This is not a book. It's an armory filled with every weapon you need to protect yourself from your own brain. Mine is a vulnerable li'l noodle. Bits of shrapnel poke Swiss cheese holes through my cerebrum, and when I saw a book that would help me stop being so mean to myself I grabbed it immediately. Kelly Balarie, save us from ourselves! Need some tactics to overcome the mental battle inside you? *Battle Ready* will equip you with every practical idea you need to be the boss of your own mind."

Melanie Dale, author of *It's Not Fair: Learning to Love the Life You Didn't Choose* and *Women Are Scary: The Totally Awkward Adventure of Finding Mom Friends*

"Though nothing can replace the Word of God to renew your mind, Kelly Balarie shares both Scripture and personal stories in a relatable way that helps increase your courage and confidence.

Battle Ready gives practical directives to show you how God wants to meet you in each struggle to help, teach, and train your soul with truth strategies that empower. If you are longing for renewal and want to experience real transformation, then this is the perfect book for you."

Gwen Smith, cofounder of Girlfriends in God, speaker, worship leader, and author of *I Want It ALL* and *Broken Into Beautiful*

"When I minister to people who are battling fear or anxiety, I will start with sharing my own 'day in the life of a bipolar' story. But then I will give them five things I do on a daily basis to thrive with it! One of those things is to read books on the subject; I will now be including *Battle Ready* in that list. First, reading is imperative when I am having a tough mental day because it allows me to get my mind off my mind. If I can sit down, get still, and dive into a book like *Battle Ready*, my mind is focusing on the words, the pages, and the inspiration, not on the anxieties and fears of that day. Second, no doubt God has called and equipped experts to pen their stories and knowledge for the betterment of others. *Battle Ready* is no exception. I look forward to giving this book away to the people I minister to and know that God will use Kelly's personal experience and His infallible Word to bring help and healing to their minds."

Heather Funk Palacios, Church by the Glades

"*Battle Ready* is a powerful and practical tool that will help you bridge the gap between your destiny and the smokescreen of mental, spiritual, and emotional attacks that oppose it to keep it from becoming reality. Powerful people think powerful thoughts! This book will empower you to think powerfully so you can live a bold and victorious life."

Justin Allen, founder, president, and apostolic overseer of Perpetual Springs Ministries, Associate of Global Awakening

"If you struggle to believe God's promises or to feel secure in your identity as His daughter, *Battle Ready* will walk you through strategies to strengthen your faith and confidence. Kelly is like a warm friend who links arms with you, offering everything she's learned in her own journey, and her honesty as she shares stories of her own battles makes this a relatable read."

Mary Carver, coauthor of *Choose Joy: Finding Hope & Purpose When Life Hurts*

"In *Battle Ready*, Kelly Balarie vulnerably shares from her struggles with runaway thoughts and self-limiting words. Her real-life action steps exhort and equip us to take control of our minds, submit our hearts to Christ, and experience a resulting life transformation. *Battle Ready* is packed with honest, heartfelt encouragement, and I can't wait to read it again."

Jen Weaver, author of *A Wife's Secret to Happiness*

"The enemy has two goals: to keep us from believing and surrendering our lives to Jesus, and, if he cannot accomplish that, to keep us rendered useless as believers, tied up in bondage, lies, and shame. Through Kelly's study, these lies and shame can be changed into truth and confidence, setting us free to be all God has designed and called us to be. God is moving to set His daughters free, and a renewing of the mind is where it starts. I believe this book is where God is working—renewing our minds to transform us into victorious warriors. I recommend all women spend time investing in their freedom, in the truth and love of God that are captured so well by Kelly in *Battle Ready*!"

Carmella Hansberger, Bible study teacher
and women's pastor at Mariners Church, Irvine, CA

BATTLE
Ready

TRAIN YOUR
MIND TO
CONQUER CHALLENGES,
DEFEAT DOUBT,
AND LIVE VICTORIOUSLY

KELLY BALARIE

BakerBooks

a division of Baker Publishing Group
Grand Rapids, Michigan

Published by Baker Books
a division of Baker Publishing Group
PO Box 6287, Grand Rapids, MI 49516-6287
www.bakerbooks.com

Printed in the United States of America

Library of Congress Cataloging-in-Publication Data
Names: Balarie, Kelly, 1978– author.
Title: Battle ready : train your mind to conquer challenges, defeat doubt, and live
    victoriously / Kelly Balarie.
Description: Grand Rapids : Baker Publishing Group, 2018. | Includes
    bibliographical references.
Identifiers: LCCN 2017061312 | ISBN 9780801019357 (pbk.)
Subjects: LCSH: Christian women—Religious life. | Thought and thinking—
    Religious aspects—Christianity. | Spiritual warfare.
Classification: LCC BV4527 .B3449 2018 | DDC 248.8/43—dc23
LC record available at https://lccn.loc.gov/2017061312

The author is represented by MacGregor Literary, Inc.

18 19 20 21 22 23 24   7 6 5 4 3 2 1

This book is dedicated to the everyday warrior woman . . . the one crying out in pain, the one shaving her head due to cancer, the one with a marriage hanging by a thread, the one suffering through an onslaught of mean words, the one trying to lift her head again, the one hoping to beat her nightly drinks, the one who calls herself a "bad mom," the one pleading for a lost loved one, the one whose past beats her up, the one who goes to church yet still feels lonely, the one who's done things horribly wrong. It is to you and to me—regular women fighting the good fight.

Contents

Introduction: Dear Reader: Yes, God Can • 17
Tips for Using This Book • 19

⇛ - - - - - **Warrior Mind-Set One** • **23** - - - - - →

There Is a Way, You Just Have to Choose to See It

(Possibility)

Bad Mind-Sets Breed Bad Mind-Sets • What God Plants, He'll Grow •
The Most Important Thing We Always Forget • If You're Lost,
This Will Help Get You Found, Fast

⇛ - - - - - **Warrior Mind-Set Two** • **41** - - - - - →

Your Identity Isn't Who You Think You Are,
It's Who He Says You Are

(Identity)

Why Your Camera Roll Tells the Whole Story • Good Lessons from a
Desperate, Dying Dog • You Can't Easily Win the Game If You Run
Tail between Your Legs from the Ball • Beware of the Snares
That Snatch Your True Identity

⟫⟫⟫ - - - - - **Warrior Mind-Set Three • 63** - - - - - →

She Who Walks with an Open, Receptive Heart
Finds It Filled by God

(Sensitivity)

Want to See God? • Ten-Second Techniques to Leverage the Power
of Your Mini-Mind • Get Your Heart-Health Checkup •
Ten Proven Strategies to Cultivate a Big Heart •
What's So Great about BIG Open Hearts

Intermission One: A Minding Grace Note

- - - - - **Warrior Mind-Set Four • 95** - - - - - -

The Difference between Complacency and Victory Is Action

(Activity)

The Awe-Inspiring Art of *Just Do It* • Six Beliefs That Compound
Complacency • Why Starting Something Doesn't Make You as Stupid
as You Feel • Ten Quick Ways to Form Long-Lasting New Habits •
Miss This and You'll Miss It All

- - - - - **Warrior Mind-Set Five • 115** - - - - - -

It's Not about How Low You Go for God as Much
as It Is How Near to His Embrace You Stay

(Humility)

A Modern-Day Woman's Epidemic: Slapping the Hand of God • The
True Reason You Always Feel Left Out • The Either-Or Decisions
That'll Bless or Distress You • Three Ways to Align Your Mind with
Christ's • Why Love Ricochets and Always Hits You Back

Contents

- - - - - **Warrior Mind-Set Six** • **139** - - - - - - -

*It's Not What Your Eyes See, but What the Eyes
of Your Heart See, That Lets You See Everything*

(Objectivity)

Six Self-Reflection Questions That Bring Clarity • Why Bad Eyesight
Perpetuates Horrible Feelings • How to Start Seeing from Jesus's
Angle • Lessons and Keys You Can Daily Hold and Leverage •
Thirty-Second Practices That Deliver Peace

Intermission Two: A Minding Grace Note

- - - - **Warrior Mind-Set Seven** • **165** - - - - - -

*Success Is as Simple as Letting God Help
You Back Up, Again and Again*

(Bounce-Back Ability)

Thoughts That Make You Hit Rock Bottom • Your CliffsNotes
Version of Life • Resilient People Remember These Ten Secrets
of Resiliency • Foundational Truths That *Always* Put You
Back on Safe Ground

- - - - **Warrior Mind-Set Eight** • **181** - - - - - -

Throw the Junk Away to Find the Gem

(Simplicity)

The Constant Battle You Fear You'll Never Win • Self-Assessment:
Learn Why You Struggle to Follow Jesus • What Looks Stupid to the
World May Look Brilliant to God • A List of Ten Things You Need to
Stop Doing ASAP • Fail to Plan, Plan to Fail

- - - - - **Warrior Mind-Set Nine** • 203 - - - - - -

The One with Her Eye on the Prize
Goes Home with the Trophy

(Eternity)

What I Was Missing (and You Might Be Too) • Practical and Radical
Heart Change Starts with This • The Most Important Thing
We're Almost Always Forgetting • Five Renewing Thoughts •
Two "If" Statements to Remember

Intermission Three: A Minding Grace Note

- - - - - **Warrior Mind-Set Ten** • 219 - - - - - -

Say "God Can, and I Will Rest in That"

(Positivity)

One Way or the Other Thinking: Move Forward or Step Back •
Ten Reasons Forward Thinking Is Mind-Altering •
The Five-Point Mind-Renew

- - - - - **Warrior Mind-Set Eleven** • 243 - - - - - -

She Who Realizes She Has Nothing to Lose
Understands She Has Everything to Gain

(Intensity)

What Matters Is What's in Your Hand • Seven Vulnerabilities the
Enemy Consistently Attacks (F.I.G.H.T.E.R.) • The 3L Battle Plan

- - - - - **Warrior Mind-Set Twelve** • **259** - - - - -

It's Not about What You Can or Can't Do,
It's Only about What He Can Do—through You

(Impossibility)

Imagine If . . . • Lies! Lies! Lies! Five Lies We Need to
Stop Believing • Why It's Okay If You Feel You're Cracking along
the Way • Faith, Meet My Friend, _____ • Last Things Last

Tying Up Loose Ends • 275
Acknowledgments • 277
Notes • 279
About the Author • 283

Introduction

Dear Reader: Yes, God Can

No, I can't.

Are you tired of your struggle? Over your feelings of frustration? Discouraged because you haven't handled things better? Unsure of what to do or where to go from here? Upset at yourself or others? Limited because of everything happening around you?

Life is a battle.

How is your fight coming?

You know, I spent years externally focusing on people, problems, and pressing issues, but it wasn't until I started to internally focus on my thoughts and beliefs that I found breakthrough.

This book is my breakthrough. It includes hard-fought and hard-won lessons, dug up during my toughest of times (arguments, health issues, extreme self-doubt, family catastrophes, an eating disorder, death in the family, deep financial debt, faith crises, taunting memories, depression, natural disaster fleeing, and so on).

It also includes tips, insights, and stories I've searched for and studied in order to learn how to make godly habits stick for good. I am sharing the best of what I have found to be the best for you.

This book is all about reclaiming, training, and coming alive to the mind of Christ, so you no longer live crippled by doubt, discouragement, or defeat.

This book's goal, for you and for me, is: yes, God can.

Love,
Kelly

Tips for Using This Book

1. **Do not view it as a study guide.** This book is less about Hebrew and Greek translations and more about saying, "Aha! I've seen this verse a hundred times, but I never saw it like *that*. This changes everything."

2. **Use it with a highlighter.** There are 301 tips here, or something like that. Easily, this book could come off as spiritual overload if done alone—without the Counselor, Redeemer, and Restorer. This would be a pity. To avoid this, pray. Pray something like: "God, stop me in my ordinary tracks as I go through this book. Let me see what You desire me to see. Father, highlight and make the points, instructions, and truths You desire I move on stand out. Pour out the grace I need to change. I trust You." Then circle, journal, scribble, or highlight what you need to. Make this book yours.

3. **Go slow.** I read books and whiz through them. This is not that type of book. This is a slow read; it is like marinating meat. Give yourself the space of time so these life-changing words can seep in. You can do this by stopping to respond to God, reading at a peace-filled pace, permitting yourself room to think and practice, and returning to this book over the years.

4. Be open. Avoid being the person who says, "I know that already." My question back to you would be, "Do you 100 percent live it already?" You know, when we've driven a road a hundred times before, we miss things— the budding daisies, the bluebird in the tree on the right side of the road, and the sun setting on the left. Sometimes it is in our *claiming to know it all* that we end up missing it all.

5. Never, ever think the work is all up to you. I've tried to change my mind on my own and to work up belief. Every time I do, I fail—miserably. You will too if you arduously try to whip up a "perfect new you." Instead, take a deep breath and relax. God has you. He has this. He will be faithful to complete the good work He is beginning in you.

6. Write out your own personal battle plan. See Warrior Mind-Set Twelve for more on this. Download your battle plan at www.iam battleready.com.

7. Get your hands dirty. This book is not a read-and-be-done kind of book. It's a get-in-and-get-your-hands-dirty kind of book. This is intentional. You need to hear something more than once to adopt it. So write and process your new thoughts. Doing these things will better ingrain what you need to know in your head.

8. Mind the "-ity" word. Each chapter boils down to one itty-bitty "-ity" word (you'll see them in the table of contents and at the beginning of each chapter). This word offers you a bottom-line summary as a point of focus for your future days. If you memorize these twelve most important words, you can take them home with you when the book is said and done.

And finally . . . This book is a manual for the mind to help you live a soul-fulfilling and love-spreading life that, at the end of your days, you can say *mattered*. I am expectant there will be great accounts of life change, hopefulness, and barrier-breaking as a result of the how-to lessons included here. Share your story about #battlereadybook at www.iambattleready.com and download a ton of freebies.

<<< DOWNLOAD >>> "7 Battle Ready Verses That Get Daughters Ready for Battle" at www .iambattleready.com.

Warrior Mind-Set One

There Is a Way, You Just Have to Choose to See It

(Possibility)

Faith is a place of mystery, where we find the courage
to believe in what we cannot see and the strength to let
go of our fear of uncertainty.

Brené Brown, *The Gifts of Imperfection*

Point 1: Bad Mind-Sets Breed Bad Mind-Sets

Life's greatest fight is within the mind.

I decided this at the supermarket not too long ago as I watched a
lady survey the meat counter. *Said lady?* She appeared nice enough.
The only issue was that she was beautiful and the exact opposite
of how I'd been feeling lately. . . .

Lately, I'd been trying to oil-slick all of my wild strands into a
contained mass of frizzless order. Lately, I'd been trying to cover
my gray roots. Lately, I'd been trying to triple-foundation-cover
redness on my cheeks that wouldn't relent. Lately, I'd been trying
to yank-button my shorts to hide an ever-bulging waistline. Lately,
I'd been scouring online reviews for wrinkle creams that actually
work (without success, I might add).

So when I saw *her*, I hated *me* even more.

Her. In all her tight-fit body glory, walking around in *those* little spandex pants and bra-like workout shirt . . . *she* silently mocked me. Her body laughed at mine. Her unsaid words critiqued me. Her confidence attacked mine. *That show off!!!* So I did what any violently threatened woman would do—I fought back.

Right there, while holding the hand of my little toddler and a bag of chips, I envisioned myself approaching her, tapping her on the shoulder, and saying, "Excuse me, dear, I just want to let you know . . . your outfit sure is cute. So cute, in fact, I don't think anyone would ever notice the bulges of back fat you probably never noticed when you looked in the mirror this morning."

Bam! I'd hit her.

Then I'd offer her a wink and be on my way. I'd march off with the military precision of a girl who *just won the war*! She'd stand there, mouth agape I'm sure . . . and I'd forget about how all those pretty girls back in third grade once made me feel.

All this? My imaginary emotional uplift? This little break from my own faults? It felt so good in the moment . . . so right. Until the regret came and I realized I had just done the unthinkable, what I'd pledged within my heart not to do: criticize, tear down, and rip apart another person.

Why do I always do what I don't want to do?

Not too long after, my son and I checked out at the counter. The cashier passed us a little red contest ticket. You get it for bringing your own bag. A chance to win $25 at the store by dropping that little red ticket in its own special box. I pointed out the box about twenty feet away and told my son to drop it in as I finished paying. The problem was, once there, my son couldn't reach it. Jumping didn't help either. Neither did my encouragement from afar. To make matters worse, *she* came. Said-lady rolled her pristine self and bagged-up cart right next to him. I believe I pretended not to look, but I certainly heard her voice, sweet like honey, say, "Hi, cutie, can I help you, little darling?"

Workout Barbie then looked over and yelled to me, "He's so cute!" She lifted him just right so he fit his little ticket in the box and affectionately dropped him down. She smiled big and waved goodbye. I wanted to hate her. I did.

But I couldn't. Turns out, she was a kind lady with back fat rolls about half the size of mine. A thousand pound weight heaped on my back.

I am so bad. I am horribly bad. I will never, ever be good.

Point 2: What God Plants, He'll Grow

This. This lady is why I wrote this book. Well, it's not just her, it's all of it: it's the way I personalize things, it's how I feel like everyone's against me, it's how I blame people, it's how I blame myself, it's how I feel like I don't do anything right, it's how I feel I won't survive when troubles hit, it's how I doubt God will pull through for me, it's how I think you're talking behind my back, it's how I feel outside God's circle of love more days than not, it's how I ditch people before they ditch me, it's how I believe good things for others but not for myself, it's the guilt and the shame, it's my fear of making mistakes . . . it's all of it.

Basically, it's the agony of all my swirling constantly yakking negativity . . .

About people
> *People hurt me.*
> *People hold me back.*
> *People are out to get me.*
> *People won't like me if I'm me.*

About myself
> *What is wrong with me?*
> *Why can't I do anything right?*
> *Why aren't I like her?*

I am unworthy.
I always mess up.

About how I act
    I never follow through.
    I always fail.
    I have too much to do.
    I have no good talents.
    I never get anywhere.
    I have limited resources.

About God
    He never pulls through for me.
    He gives others better gifts.
    He leaves me all on my own.
    He doesn't care.
    He doesn't want me if I mess up.
    He is unforgiving and angry.

About pain, problems, and purpose
    The world is against me.
    My finances will never improve.
    God created me to suffer.
    It's all useless anyway.
    God always allows trouble to find me.

This supermarket fiasco just brought the facts to light: *the thoughts I sow create the life I reap.* I sowed mean thoughts about Barbie-beauty, so I glared at her with contempt. But if I sowed thoughts of love, what could I have reaped? A new friend? A moment of joy as I connected with her? A passing glance that acknowledged how being a mom is hard? We reap what we sow.

"The one who sows righteousness reaps a sure reward" (Prov. 11:18). To sow seeds of bad thinking or unrighteousness almost always reaps a harvest of bad consequences: distance from God, hatred toward oneself, frustration at life, irritation at a lack of growth. Looking back, I can see how this has played out time and time again in my life.

So often . . .

I sowed the thought: *I can't do it.*

As a result, I've failed nearly dozens of business ideas: I attempted to start a local chef party that rotated houses. *Fail.* I studied to become a realtor. *Fail.* I desired to be a psychologist. *Fail.* I left a company to start my own. *Fail.* I got the idea to be a life coach. *Fail.*

Fail. Fail. And more failing. Each fail built on the last fail, building a track record of failingness that proved: *I'm a failure.*

I reaped: An identity of a failure.

I sowed the thought: *[Insert name] is thinking [XYZ] about me. They must [hate, not like, think poorly of, not want, be judging] me.*

I remember passing a common friend at a gathering. She didn't smile at me; she didn't even look at me. She just walked right on by—looking completely the other way. *She's rude,* I thought. Then, *She must hate me. I must have done something to her—and not even realized it. I am always messing up relationships.*

For the rest of the event, all I thought about was her: avoiding her, reading into her facial expressions, and smiling at her when she came near. I was consumed with my own insecurity.

Only later did I come to learn she was near a breaking point that night with emotional issues that felt internally crushing. She was ashamed and so head-down she walked into the gathering. Her issue never was about me.

I reaped: Insecurity that blinds the eyes of ministry. It steals fun.

I sowed the thought: *I exist to just "get by."*

Rather than focusing on what was soul-important, I got focused on what the world declared "so important": to-do lists, carpools, errands, perfection, appearances, and busyness. I lived life frazzled, fast-paced, rushed, haphazard, and soulless. With anxiety. Underneath, I knew I couldn't do it all.

I reaped: Continual anxiety and fear of being exposed as a fraud.

I sowed the thought: *I am so stupid.*

I remember reversing out of our driveway. I crushed the back of the car into our mailbox. All I could think was, *You idiot. Why are you always so dumb?*

I reaped: A paralyzed life. My self-restricting words trained my mind not to move forward with opportunities, risks, and dreams.

I sowed the thought: *I can't trust people (or God); they hurt me.*

In grade school, I cheated—in Bible class. I didn't put my pen down. I was "the idiot" still writing. I did this, even though the teacher had specifically told me pre-exam, "God knows the cheaters. He sees all the bad things you do." The teacher had me rip up the test and trash it. He threatened to throw the trash out the window in front of the whole class.

I reaped: Shame. I can't mess up or ever do bad things because I'll be the embarrassed fool.

I sowed the thought: *People will never like me for who I am.*

I regularly met with a group of women on Tuesdays to do a book club. And while I loved the subject matter, I was horribly afraid to talk. I didn't want to come off too strong or too pushy or too [whatever]. So I hid and protected myself from their thoughts of *She's too [arrogant, confident, proud, knowledgeable]*.

I reaped: Lies about who I really was.

I sowed the thought: *Life's unfair to me and always will be.*

When I found out my condo in California was a mold-infested hotbed, I freaked. I searched the internet nearly twenty-four hours a day trying to find solutions, I sent petri dishes with moldy home tests to far-off places, and I counted every loss in terms of money, health, and future happiness. God cared for the poor and hungry in Ethiopia—not for me.

I reaped: A crisis-mode life where God doesn't show up.

Amazingly, because of the chemical makeup of our brain, our mind deciphers no difference between perception and reality. What we think instructs our mind. Repeated negative statements, sowed day after day, tell our mind, "Hey, that right there is *my* truth!" Then our mind acts on it—whether we like it or not.

Thoughts sowed reap habits. Habits create your life.

Be careful, little mind, what you think. Your thoughts can either push you ahead or draw you back, restrict you or re-create you, antagonize you or harmonize you with God's peace.

What do you sow? What do you reap? What are you seeing in your life?

"Blessed . . . are those who hear the word of God and obey it" (Luke 11:28). **Sow** a hearing of real truth, **reap** obedience, and **see** God's blessing.

SOW > > > REAP > > > SEE

Take an inventory of what you see in your life. Check all that apply:

☐ Do you ever get the burning sense you shouldn't be so discouraged, doubtful, or disheveled?

☐ Do you hate the fact that you know God's truths but hardly live them?

□ Do you silently berate yourself for failing once again?

□ Do you see all you don't do right, or just ignore them altogether?

□ Do you blame people, the past, or predicaments to justify your subpar life?

□ Do you spend long spans of time feeling sorry for yourself?

□ Do you let other people dictate your whereabouts or your life?

□ Does the idea of change scare you?

□ Do you get worried about things you can't control?

□ Do you sign up for too much, say yes to everything, and then find you can do nothing?

□ Do you hate the woman who is ten times more perfect, pretty, or put-together than you?

□ Do you have hopes and dreams you can't access? Or that have been "in the works" for over a year?

□ Do you give up after setbacks, critiques, or difficulty?

□ Do you shy away from opportunities because you aren't "good enough"?

□ Do you sit around waiting for God to change something/ someone so you can finally be happy?

□ Do you do okay in life until semblances of a storm sneak up on you and threaten to steal everything?*

Point 3: The Most Important Thing We Always Forget

Consider your mind as a smartphone. Let's call it your MindPhone, if you will.

It is what you carry with you, what you rely on, what you use to keep your day straight, what makes you remember stuff, what gives you information, what brings order, what brings to remembrance

---

*To learn more about your personal journey, story, and thought processes, don't miss the "Examine Your Story" sections at the end of each chapter.

old memories, what you keep referring to, what dictates the kind of life you want to live . . . your MindPhone is your life. It orders everything.

It also is programmable, compartmentalized, and maintained almost entirely by you. Imagine that. You are the boss of it.

Now, what may surprise you is, without realizing it—over many years—you've customized your MindPhone. You've put messages into it. Messages from the world, TV, friends, and family; God's truths; labels from the past; demands of others; inner thoughts and repetitive phrases; things you see and ideas you have; perceptions both real and unreal; and world outlooks.

As I have observed, those who plow evil and those who sow trouble reap it. (Job 4:8)

Input: negativity

Sow: a generalized sense that everything is working against you

See: a mouth that speaks cynicism, criticism, gloom, worry, or anxiety

Input: constant irritation with others

Sow: a mind that dwells on grievances

See: an isolated and lonely life because you're "good and done with all of them"

Input becomes output in a life.

INPUT > > > OUTPUT
REAP > > > SOW
SOW > > > WHAT YOU SEE

What you feed your mind matters. You see, feedings turn into your feelings: a sense of being overwhelmed because you've got thirty text messages, anxiety after hanging out with critical friends, a wavering belief in God because you don't spend time with Him.

This. All this. This is a silent epidemic: we fail to mind our mind.

Instead, we walk around in a haphazard mess of busyness, disorganization, and fast-paced happenings, forgetting where we placed *what matters most*. Yet what we search for is right in our back pocket, waiting to be renewed.

Our mind is the MindPhone we keep misplacing. Even more, our thoughts are usually spam. Seriously. We have no filter. Piled high and overloaded, our mind mailbox gets filled with icky, old, negative, and unproductive messages. It doesn't have to be this way. Just because it comes in doesn't mean we have to keep it.

Throughout this book, we will embrace a new way:

[FILTER] + [DELETE] = LIVING BY THE MIND OF CHRIST

Point 4: If You're Lost, This Will Help Get You Found, Fast

Failing to mind your mind does hurt you. I want you to consider this: if you have a phone but throw it out, it serves no purpose. If you get too busy to look at it, it won't help you. If you place it on a shelf in your closet, it'll collect dust.

If you pay no attention to your MindPhone, it won't do much. Great, untapped potential will go largely unused. The mind of Christ, the precious gift Jesus gave, won't incredibly change your life. And the Word of God likely won't become the words you live by.

In other words, at the end of the day, you'll feel inside: *I've blown it.*

Maybe, like me, this is precisely how you feel right now—like you've blown it or used your mind against yourself. That's okay. Starting now, things are about to change.

We are going to dust off our MindPhone to discover what it was made for, what it can do, what God says it is all about. Take a look.

God intends that his daughters:

Focus on Jesus and prepare to be changed.
"Don't become so well-adjusted to your culture that you fit into it without even thinking. Instead, *fix your attention on God.* You'll be changed from the inside out. Readily recognize what he wants from you, and quickly respond to it. Unlike the culture around you, always dragging you down to its level of immaturity, God brings the best out of you, develops well-formed maturity in you" (Rom. 12:1–2 MSG, emphasis added).

Seize the fact: we are free, free, free!
"So if the Son sets you free, you will be free indeed" (John 8:36).

100 percent believe: we have His mind.
"We have the mind of Christ" (1 Cor. 2:16).

Be transformed.
"Do not conform to the pattern of this world, but be transformed by the renewing of your mind" (Rom. 12:2).

Take our thoughts captive.
"We demolish arguments and every pretension that sets itself up against the knowledge of God, and we take captive every thought to make it obedient to Christ" (2 Cor. 10:5).

Discover His perfect will.
"Then you will be able to test and approve what God's will is—his good, pleasing and perfect will" (Rom. 12:2).

Seek His righteousness and believe He is adding "all these things" to us.
"But seek first his kingdom and his righteousness, and all these things will be given to you as well" (Matt. 6:33).

God purposes that we:

Move from the slavery of shame to the liberty of grace.
"For sin shall no longer be your master, because you are not under the law, but under grace" (Rom. 6:14).

Live as conquerors, not constant condemners of self.
"No, in all these things we are more than conquerors through [Jesus] who loved us" (Rom. 8:37).

Strengthen in faith and love.
"I pray that out of his glorious riches he may strengthen you with power through his Spirit in your inner being, so that Christ may dwell in your hearts through faith" (Eph. 3:16–17).

Embrace God with the fullness of our "mind" (Greek translation: imagination, understanding).
"'Love the Lord your God with all your heart and with all your soul and with all your mind.' This is the first and greatest commandment. And the second is like it: 'Love your neighbor as yourself'" (Matt. 22:37–39).

Fix our hope on grace.
"Therefore, prepare your minds for action, keep sober in spirit, fix your hope completely on the grace to be brought to you at the revelation of Jesus Christ" (1 Pet. 1:13 NASB).

Walk in Christ's victory.
"But thanks be to God! He gives us the victory through our Lord Jesus Christ" (1 Cor. 15:57).

Be transformed, and then transform the world.
"For as he thinketh in his heart, so is he" (Prov. 23:7 KJV).

Call this your "Intents and Purposes Map App." It tells you where you're going. This is important because it

- reminds you of where God is taking you.
- presents a glimpse into the inner workings of the Master Developer of your mind.
- offers you a top-down rather than bottom-up view.
- sets the destination while allowing God to prompt your routes.
- keeps you from hazards that intend to get you lost.

A girl with a "Map App" doesn't easily get lost. She sees where she's going and uncompromisingly heads there.

Now, I realize this may not be the case today. You may feel you've lost your mind to sadness, loneliness, self-hatred, annoyance, pessimism, or apathy, but you haven't. No mind is too impossibly lost for Jesus.

"The Son of Man came to seek and to save the lost" (Luke 19:10). This means nothing is too impossibly lost for Jesus. Jesus finds the lost sheep, heals the sick woman, makes the blind see, and restores dignity. With Jesus, what is impossibly lost gets found. This is the saving nature of a Savior. All impossibilities are possible with Christ.

So pull out that MindPhone. It is time for some reprogramming. So much of the amazing possibility in you is about to get found.

<<< WATCH >>> a free mini-video session called "5 Simple Thoughts That Will Change Your Day" with Kelly Balarie. Gain encouragement for this journey. Find it at: www.iambattleready.com.

Reap = Sow

REMEMBER TO MIND YOUR MIND

BEWARE OF SPAM THOUGHTS

ALL THINGS ARE POSSIBLE WITH JESUS

A MIND TO CONQUER

Prepare today, for tomorrow may be the
greatest battle of your life.

Check out Ephesians 6:13–18:

> Be prepared. You're up against far more than you can handle on
> your own. Take all the help you can get, every weapon God has
> issued, so that when it's all over but the shouting you'll still be on
> your feet. Truth, righteousness, peace, faith, and salvation are more
> than words. Learn how to apply them. You'll need them throughout
> your life. God's Word is an *indispensable* weapon. In the same way,
> prayer is essential in this ongoing warfare. Pray hard and long.
> Pray for your brothers and sisters. Keep your eyes open. Keep each
> other's spirits up so that no one falls behind or drops out. (MSG)

PRAY

God, train us by Your Word and teach us according to Your
heart. Your Word is our weapon, and prayer is our best de-
fense. Inspire constant prayer. Help us to pray for our other
sisters, the ones we can't see reading this book, the ones jour-
neying just like us. May no woman be left behind. May our
mutual prayers rise up in support of each other, may we feel
Your help, and may the great mission of mind-renewal come
forth in Your perfect timing. Grant us great understanding
that we are not in this alone. In Jesus's name we pray. Amen.

WRITE THREE THINGS YOU'RE THANKFUL FOR

1. _____

2. _____

3. _____

ENTER YOUR MIND

You should know a little bit more about your MindPhone before we really get going. Primarily, neuroplasticity is a good thing: it means that just as plastic is moldable and changeable under heat, so is your mind. You can rework it, remold it. Especially in the heat of a hard-fought battle.

- The possibilities of your mind are endless: A study reveals the capacity in your brain is enough for the whole internet.[1]
- 77 percent of what people think is negative, and we hear "I said no" in our households an average of 148,000 times before we reach age eighteen.[2]
- Negativity is contagious. What people say affects us into our future days.[3]

Rick Hanson, author of *Hardwiring Happiness*, says, "Staying with a negative experience past the point that's useful is like running laps in Hell: You dig the track a little deeper in your brain each time." But, "By taking just a few extra seconds to stay with a positive experience—even the comfort in a single breath—you'll help turn a passing mental state into lasting neural structure."[4]

What would it look like for you to "stay" with the positive? To keep pondering it? When would you need to do this?

EXAMINE YOUR STORY

Recently I went into a coffee shop. The barista asked me how my day was. I answered, "It could be better. I 'went off' on my kids again." Frankly, it was a bad day.

She gazed into my eyes with sympathy and replied, "Power is learning we don't actually have bad days, just bad moments."

Her words stuck. I've let bad moments become a declaration over my day—my life, even. Yet freedom is saying, "I am struggling in this moment, but God can do a powerful thing in the next. His grace is enough for me, right here, right now."

1. What sets you off? Write down the kind of situations, triggers, or comments that really get your mind moving downhill.

2. What precision and perfection do you demand from yourself in life?

3. Write a list of what thoughts you tend to reap through your day. Write down the exact words that go through your head.

4. How might you consider offering yourself Christ's hard-fought "bad moment" forgiveness?

5. Next to each thought you wrote down, write what you might sow in your life, if you continue with them ad nauseam.

EXPLORE WITH GROUP STUDY

1. What did you learn from your personal study time?

2. Do you believe you can change? Why or why not?

3. When you close this book, what do you hope to gain? Take a moment to pray for each other in terms of what you each desire most.

4. Read 1 Samuel 3:1–14.

   • How has God been trying to get your attention so you will pay attention to your mind?

   • Like Samuel, how is your heart prone to miss God? How can you "catch this" in your life?

   • What did Eli tell Samuel to say to God?

   • How do you believe this phrase might change your mind? How might it foster God's best things?

   • What are some ways God might be prompting you to increase your receptivity and connectivity to Him as you progress through this book?

5. What intent and purpose of God's is most difficult to believe (refer to pages 33–34)? Pick one. How might clinging to this very truth reframe your battle? Encourage you?

6. Who does the battle belong to?

7. Insert the missing phrases from Psalm 18:31–36:

> For who is God besides the LORD?
>   And who is the ___ except our God?
> It is God who ___ me with strength
>   and keeps my way ___.
> ___ ___ my feet like the feet of a deer;
>   he ___ me to stand on the heights.
> ___ ___ my hands for battle;
>   my arms ___ ___ a bow of bronze.
> You make your saving help my ___,
>   and your right hand ___ me;
>   your help has ___ ___ ___.
> You ___ a broad path for my feet,
>   so that my ankles do not give way.

8. Name ways and Bible verses that prove God has control. What does this mean for your journey through this book?

A CHRIST-CENTERED PRINCIPLE GOD BLESSES

A belief that God can do more than you ask or imagine.

Looking at them, Jesus said, "With man this is impossible, but not with God; all things are possible with God." (Mark 10:27)

⫸----- Warrior Mind-Set Two -----▶

Your Identity Isn't Who You Think You Are, It's Who He Says You Are

(Identity)

> We're going to have to let truth scream louder to our souls than the lies that have infected us.
>
> Beth Moore, *So Long, Insecurity*

Point 1: Why Your Camera Roll Tells the Whole Story

We're diving into the deep end at the beginning, new friends, with an activity that I believe will reveal much about what inspires your thoughts.

I want you, for a moment, to see your MindPhone for what it is. The good. The bad. The ugly.

I also want you to physically and literally grab your actual phone and open your photo gallery. Scroll through the images. (Hopefully you have images spanning the course of at least a year. If not, go back to your reserves and look at older images.)

What do you see? How is your face? What thoughts consumed you as you took different photos? As you posed for them?

41

What were you thinking . . .

That time when you got that horrible skin rash?
I always get sick. I am a walking illness. No one wants to be near someone ugly like me.

Or when you pretended to be happy, with a big ol' smile in that photo with your children?
I am not likable. I am overbearing. I am unlovable.

Or that time it was just you, taking a selfie?
I am ugly. I am worthless. No one will ever like me.

Or when your husband had his arm around you at that nice dinner?
He couldn't really love someone as messed up as me. I am an embarrassment. I don't make him proud.

Or when you were in the kitchen, wearing an apron?
I messed up today. I can't fool anyone. They all know I am a fraud. And this dinner is all burnt.

Or that time you posed with your girlfriends after a downpour of a day downtown?
I am unlikable. I look the worst out of everyone. I always blurt out the dumbest things.

Did you notice certain "trigger" situations that set you off? That caused your mind to fall?

Our camera roll speaks to us. It tells us what's in us. It reveals the vast inner workings of our endless outer problems. It contains our facial expressions resulting from a wide variety of situations.

What do you see?

I see a glimpse into our identity. Like a gallery on a wall, this camera roll tells a story. It presents unsaid dialogues of times past, and feelings buried over, while bringing credence to the thousand words we'd never speak—or admit.

What good thought dialogue did you find as you looked back at holiday pictures and everyday happenings? Write your words down:

I am _____.

I always _____.

People feel _____ about me.

I am really _____.

God is doing _____ in my life.

God thinks I am _____.

What poor thinking did you uncover? Write down some of the thoughts you had at those times:

I am _____.

I always _____.

People feel _____ about me.

I won't ever _____.

I'll never be _____ enough.

God thinks I am _____.

God _____ me.

What did you find? If you are never seen in the photos . . . why? Notice things. What lines of thought accompany different situational triggers? What relationships add to life? Deplete life? Why? Sometimes a spam filter isn't only for stopping a thought from entering but for stopping yourself from repeatedly entering a bad situation with the same mind-set.

Fun times. Good times. A happy face. An anxious heart. Embarrassment. Self-hatred. Rejection. Anger.

Note it all. Let it exist. You may have the inclination to take the image in your hands and mentally shred it. Don't. Ripping up doesn't repeal the past. There is nothing worse you can do. When you trash what God desires to heal, only *you* are stuck with the icky, lingering remains. They don't wash off.

Let learning take hold. Learning is the start of transforming your mind. Allow it.

- Acknowledge you feel weak.
- Make a list of your "I am ___" statements.
- Note any other negative statements you need to list.
- Ask God to reveal new names for you through Scripture, prayer, and seeking (such as beloved, approved, holy).
- Be kind. Imagine, for a moment, you're your own life coach. Throughout this book, talk to yourself like you would a woman you care for. Create distance from the issue. Be constructive while also being truthful, uplifting, and encouraging to yourself.
- Speak kindness, belief, empowerment, and truth. Take note of what revives your heart. Write notes on how, in another situation just like those, you can help yourself to remember these truths (we'll learn more on this soon).

Do not:

Shame yourself.

Berate yourself.

Action-plan yourself.

Criticize yourself.

Say, "I am horrible. I am the worst. I am an idiot. I am never going to succeed. . . ."

God doesn't talk to you this way, so why should you?

I was struck recently by learning about Tom Brady. For those non-football ladies like myself, he has won more division titles than any other quarterback. It's a huge feat at his so-called old football age. I was curious how he did it. How does someone who is too old, too done, and too beat up win? Turns out he read a book called *The Inner Game of Tennis*.[1] It explains how, by removing debilitating self-judgment and critique, a mind can more readily and easily adapt to positive change and results. Our mind thrives under freedom.

"So now there is no condemnation for those who belong to Christ Jesus. And because you belong to him, the power of the life-giving Spirit has freed you from the power of sin that leads to death" (Rom. 8:1–2 NLT).

We don't need to beat ourselves up for every mistake, self-chide, boo our flub-ups, set super-high levels of unreachable goals, circle our fat, or righteously demand we self-improve or be counted out. On the contrary, we do nothing except permit room for God's love and truth to heal us and lead us.

To permit room is to say:

1. I am sorry, God. Truly sorry for (XYZ).
2. I am waiting for You, God. You will be faithful to help me.
3. I don't know how to change me, but You do, God.
4. I want to let go of my voice so I can start to hear Yours, Father.

We can wait on God's work and transformation without harshly arbitrating our every waking move. At first, this lack of self-judgment may feel odd. That's okay. Do a new thing.

Be still, and know that I am God. (Ps. 46:10)

Wait for the LORD; be strong and take heart and wait for the LORD. (Ps. 27:14)

Call to me and I will answer you and tell you great and unsearchable things you do not know. (Jer. 33:3)

Do what you've never done before to see what you've never seen before.

REAP >>> SOW >>> SEE
(JOY, PEACE, HOPE, ETC.)

"Remain in my love. . . . I have told you this so that my joy may be in you and that your joy may be complete" (John 15:9, 11).

It's like the first few days of vacation. After tackling all the to-dos, family stuff, work, laundry, cleaning, and preparing . . . once you get to your destination, it can feel hard to settle in, to settle down. But you still go with it, because you know relaxation is on the other side of day three.

Our mind needs time to settle into a new way of thinking too. We do this by being with God, without internal tirades. We take a "mind vacation" so that by day three or thirty or sixty we relax into God's thoughts, not our instinctive ones. There is wisdom in stepping back from the extreme burdens of what is not profitable.

Changes come easier. Steps become apparent. We hear God more clearly. His words come alive. Everything doesn't feel so drastic. We move lengths from our problem to see the heights of our God working in the depths of our heart.

From the perspective of a mind vacation, what might God be nudging you to stop repeating, rehashing, or reliving even if you've always believed it to be true? How might doing this help you experience God's love afresh?

> But when God, our kind and loving Savior God, stepped in, he saved us from all that. It was all his doing; we had nothing to do with it. He gave us a good bath, and we came out of it new people, washed inside and out by the Holy Spirit. (Titus 3:4–6 MSG)

If it is God's kindness that saves and cleanses us, why do we, in haste, keep speaking mean to ourselves? If God is kind, shouldn't we be that way too?

Point 2: Good Lessons from a Desperate, Dying Dog

When I look back at my old photos, I can't help but zoom in on my old dog, Argus. The poor guy, a Chesapeake Bay Retriever, was struck with a lumpy, grapefruit-sized cancer of the face; he also stank worse than month-old trash in 100-degree temperatures. As much as I adored him and he adored me, when I took my daily run, I had to leave him behind. His body couldn't handle it anymore and I wanted to run, not walk.

I would strategize my escape when leaving for a jog: *If I go out the front door, he'll show up to put dirty paw marks all over my white tee. But if I go out the side door I can run behind the barn and he'll have to rest.*

Most days I succeeded. I'd run back down the driveway and he'd stare at me from that big front window. I'm sure he was thinking, *How'd she pull a fast one on me this time?* I pranced in like I won (which I did).

But one day, sick old Argus pulled a fast one on me. It was a day I'll never forget. That day, as I attempted to escape down the fence line, I saw him hobble-running down the lane. He moved like a limping Benjie, pools of slow-motion slobber sloshing out each side of his grin. This time *he got me.*

It touched my heart. This day, Argus didn't run as if it were the last of his sick days; he ran as if it were the height of his glory days. Eagerness and passion oozed out of him. But, most of all, he was just happy to be near me, the one he loved.

He didn't leave my side. Argus stuck with me, like the best of companions, as I ran my two-mile loop. If he fell, he got up again. As if it never happened.

Argus knew whose he was. He wasn't a stray or a wild animal; he belonged to me. Love defined him, not his weakness, his limp. Joy was found near the master.

Argus knew whose he was. Do we?

We are "not our own," we've been bought "at a price" (1 Cor. 6:19–20).

We belong to God. The One who cares for us. The One who sees how hard it is. The One who stays with us.

Our Daddy's love never fails. In fact, it pushes us on.

With His love, we gain strength to run any distance. Just consider Argus. Because of love, he beat his mind that likely said, *You can't do this.* He didn't focus on being crippled but came alive. He was powerful. He wasn't dying but thriving and moving, almost like he'd never moved before. God's love compels us to "our greater." Even if our mind initially says, *No, we can't,* when we consider Jesus's mind of great sacrifice and love we're reminded, *Yes, in Christ, we can.*

What about you? Do you live like Argus, next to your Master? Or do you live alone, stuck, while life is passing you by?

Consider where you stand (check the box if you've thought this):

Stuck, life-passin'-them-by Christians think:

- ☐ *I must constantly manage my day.*
- ☐ *I must fend for myself; no one else will.*
- ☐ *No one cares for me.*
- ☐ *I'm often abandoned and left behind.*
- ☐ *I must prove I am worthy, valuable, and respectable.*
- ☐ *God can't like me for who I am.*
- ☐ *Figuring out how to be good enough for God will finally bring me joy.*
- ☐ *I can't handle it all; I don't know what to do.*
- ☐ *I must please everyone or they won't like me.*
- ☐ *Other people are judgmental and critical.*
- ☐ *God's Word constantly makes me feel like a failure.*
- ☐ *If I don't do it, no one will.*
- ☐ *I am no good.*

☐ *Everything bad happens to me.*

☐ *People cause me to sin and mess up my life.*

☐ *I am not as good as she is.*

Expectant, life-found-in-His-love companions think:

☐ *I'm just living out God's day.*

☐ *God is defending and advocating for me.*

☐ *I have the body of Christ, brothers and sisters whom God provided as spiritual support and encouragement.*

☐ *Jesus earned my worth at the cross.*

☐ *God created me as I am, and He will use me as I am.*

☐ *Being with God is my greatest joy.*

☐ *God is handling it all on my behalf; He knows just what to do.*

☐ *As I pray to God, He'll lead me—whether I give a yes or a no.*

☐ *God is gracious, kind, and slow to anger.*

☐ *God's Word reminds me of how much is available to me through Him.*

☐ *If God doesn't do it, I don't want it.*

☐ *The Spirit of God in me is very good and helps me in all my ways.*

☐ *God is with me, He is helping me, and my pain today will become wisdom tomorrow.*

☐ *If Daddy is for me, who can be against me?*

Stuck, life-passin'-them-by Christians feel outside God's circle of trust. They feel shunned by Him. They think He is angry, unforgiving, unjust, forgetful, or abandoning. They believe they always have to do lots of stuff, whining, hard work, and self-punishment, or they must constantly nag at themselves to be "good enough for Him." They regularly question if He cares. They live in angst. They may not even realize it. They've grown accustomed to it.

They tend to believe, *God isn't really as good as I pretend He is. He doesn't really care that much about me.*

Expectant, life-found-in-His-love companions realize they are secure and part of the Master's beloved family. They accept His love. They believe, "Surely God is with [me]" (Isa. 45:14).

Which camp do you find yourself in? Knowingly or unknowingly? Camp "left behind" or camp "cared for"?

May I tell you something? We're neither. We're not stuck and we're not just companions. We're *daughters.*

> Because you are his sons, God sent the Spirit of his Son into our hearts, the Spirit who calls out, "*Abba,* Father." So you are no longer a slave, but God's child; and since you are his child, God has made you also an heir. (Gal. 4:6–7)

Your identity is *God's daughter.*

Do you know what this means? If you ask God for bread, He won't give you a stone. Why? Because what good parent would do this? None. When my daughter is hungry, I run to find her favorite fruit, a nectarine. When she really wants to look pretty, I search through her closet for something special. When my son searches the ground, hunting for a hidden quarter, I toss one down when he's not looking. I try to give them not just the good gift but the best gift.

God is not withholding His goodness from you, either. He is a giver, but sometimes His best giving comes after hard living. Likewise, sometimes I parent my children in a way that transforms their heart right after severe hurt has befallen them. I don't set out to hurt them, but I still use the situation for their good. The main point is, I nearly always aim to have their "best" good in mind.

> If you, then, though you are evil, know how to give good gifts to your children, how much more will your Father in heaven give good gifts to those who ask him! (Matt. 7:11)

What if you actually started to believe God has good gifts for you because you are His beloved daughter?

Pray with me:

> *God, I fully submit to Jesus as my Lord and Savior. I thank You that He has taken my every sin. I ask Your Spirit to come alive in me, inspire me, and lead me. I want to know the love You speak of. I want to understand how much of a daughter I am. Will You help me to know You as a good Daddy? Will you show me how I am Your daughter? Will You care for me? Will You increase my visibility of the work of the Holy Spirit within me, so I may receive it and unleash Your love in full?*

To experience God's love is to begin to unleash your truest identity. "Love never fails" (1 Cor. 13:8).

Point 3: You Can't Easily Win the Game If You Run Tail between Your Legs from the Ball

When I played sports as a kid, I was a tentative player. If you threw a ball at me, I'd kind of duck out of the way, lest it hit me at nearly a hundred miles an hour and snap my nose in half, which ironically ended up happening on a field many years ago. Another story for another day . . .

What I aim to convey is I halfway wanted to catch the ball but doubted my ability to receive it.

We do the same: we one-third believe God's truth is meant for us and two-thirds believe we aren't good enough, valuable enough, holy enough, wise enough, churchy enough, strong enough, or [fill in the blank] enough to receive it. So we don't.

We act all strong and speak all strong, saying, "I got it! I got it! It's mine. I believe . . ." all the while subtly shrinking back just enough to watch it drop, dead, right before us.

Truth not grasped in a heart never works. It drops dead. It's written but not owned. It's spoken but then forgotten. Remembered but then blocked. You get the picture.

Good intentions, neglected, lead nowhere.

So, how do we learn to catch what God is doing and saying within our heart, rather than watching life pass us by?

- Paramount: we pray for greater faith to believe.
- We ask God to reveal His will for our life, so we can follow it unwaveringly.
- We believe and expect what no eye has seen, nor ear heard: the things God has planned for those who love Him (1 Cor. 2:9).
- We look for God's power in our places of weakness.
- We hear Jesus's voice in Scripture as He is talking to us.
- We place God's voice above voices of doubt.
- We allow biblical stories to become a stage-like play in our mind.
- We agree with Scripture's wisdom, even if it contradicts ours.
- We come back to what God is revealing, rather than being lured away by what's distracting.
- We are ever vigilant during times of blessings, lest they lead us away from God like our worst trials.
- We believe God sees and understands the season we are in and responds accordingly.
- We believe God's truth addresses our every life situation.
- We decide, even if we feel lost, that God is helping us to be found in Him.
- We remind ourselves daily that every Word of God is real, working, active, liberating, loving, moving, and directing.
- We know life can look different than originally expected and still be beautiful.
- We stand on God as if He's our only lifeline, which He is.

Bottom line: we make the abstract absolute.

And we think like a beloved daughter would, which sounds like this:

1. I really am God's gal!

We think:

>*Even if, for a moment, I feel lost—I am still His.*
>
>*Even when I go astray, He still finds me.*
>
>*Even when I get down, I can look up.*
>
>*Even if I hate myself, God never does.*

2. Jesus's work can never be undone!

We remember:

>*The Spirit in me (who raised Jesus from the dead) can beat anything coming against me.*
>
>*If Jesus calls me friend, indeed I am; I can talk, walk, and live with Him accordingly.*
>
>*I am not partially forgiven; I am fully chosen, wanted, and loved, all days, all the time.*

3. Close to God, I come close to seeing who He created me to be!

We go back to:

>*The only place I find my true image is in the reflection of Christ.*
>
>*Contentment is living with God and full of God.*
>
>*I'm unstoppable when I stop hesitating and live on mission with God.*
>
>*If He is calling me to it, He'll enable me to do it.*

We let feelings fall where they may and simply catch God's truth. That's it. We run holding on to that and only that. Because otherwise the game never changes and everything stays the same. Or we lose.

Victory, on the other hand, is catching God's truth and owning it, right up against your heart. It is reciting it aloud. Repeating it like a broken record. Ditching spam if it doesn't line up to truth. And returning back to a thirty-second prayer, once or a hundred times a day, to be rearmed with Christ's promises.

Victory is offense on repeat.

Offense that looks like adjusting your stance, abandoning the inner meanie, and dwelling on the hard-fought-for identities of daughter, beloved, chosen, righteous, God's workmanship, partaker in God's divine nature, complete in Christ, holy, blameless, sealed, renewed, remade, restored, provided for, filled, equipped, enabled, empowered by the Holy Spirit, given the mind of Christ, transformed into Christ's ambassadors, royal priesthood, image, holy nation, and temple.

Victory doesn't cross her arms on the field; she opens them so love, joy, peace, patience, kindness, goodness, gentleness, faithfulness, and self-control are caught right where she is. Daddy's best falls on her.

She catches it.

Point 4: Beware of the Snares That Snatch Your True Identity

A snare is anything with the potential to trip you up. With your face planted in the ground, you can't see yourself. Likewise, there are mind-sets, attitudes, and demands that often prevent us from seeing who we really are. We want to clear those out of the way early in this book, so that our true self can emerge. Be aware of these:

1. **This book is a great opportunity.** Choose to forget the "must-dos" and "have-tos;" those die out easy. Think: "with-God-I-get-to," "It's-an-honor-to," and "God-is-calling-me-to." These type of thoughts both empower you and open up new doors, which you will see through.

2. **Heavenly God is not your earthly father.** How do you see your father? What qualities, strong or weak, would you give him? Research shows our view of our earthly father tends to be what we see in our heavenly one. What have you, perhaps subconsciously, come to believe about God? (Examples: God is judgmental, critical, stubborn, far away, angry, mean, etc.)

3. **God's not looking for all-star valedictorians but heart-led companions who are loyal.** "For the eyes of the LORD range throughout the earth to strengthen those whose hearts are fully committed to him" (2 Chron. 16:9). God wants your heart more than He wants your work. Continually return to this point.

4. **Don't demand your mind change in no time.** People don't get a PhD in a day. Our higher learning takes time. Give yourself a break. It actually takes sixty-six days to form a new habit.

5. **Don't settle for a crumb from the pantry when God is giving you access to His spiritual storehouses.** If God gave us His Son, "How will he not also, along with him, graciously give us all things?" (Rom. 8:32).

6. You're not selfish or self-indulgent for shining God's glory. "Those who look to him are radiant; their faces are never covered with shame" (Ps. 34:5). Don't be ashamed if, as you go through this book, you start to feel radiant. Shine. God fully intends your light to shine (see Matt. 5:16).

7. **Remember the party!** The character of God is not a killjoy; Jesus knew how to have a good time (see the wedding at Cana in John 2). With this, don't feel guilty for celebrating your photo galleries of progress. It is not a sin to be happy. I believe God cheers on all your progress; He delights in progress.

8. **Don't ignore your patterns.** I've noticed that by repeatedly doing the opposite of my negative pattern, I break it. I break

off who I was never intended to be and I find God's true intent for me.

Keep these reminders near you. Also keep near the truth that this book is a daily battle. It seems to live practically three steps forward, two steps back. Avoid getting discouraged by backward movement. Two steps back often provide the needed space to take a running leap into God's next best thing. God will be faithful. He is known to do "immeasurably more" than we can ask or imagine (Eph. 3:20). Daughters know this. Daddy always has a heart to help.

And after you have suffered a little while, the God of all grace, who has called you to his eternal glory in Christ, will himself restore, confirm, strengthen, and establish you. (1 Pet. 5:10 ESV)

<<< REMIND >>> yourself of who you are. Get "12 Printable Identity Notecards." Post them to remind you who you are. Download at www.iambattleready.com.

Learning = Progress

MIND VACATIONS ARE FREEDOM

LIVE LIKE A DAUGHTER

GOOD INTENTIONS, NEGLECTED,
LEAD NOWHERE

A MIND TO CONQUER

If you don't know who you are,
you'll tend to be everyone—but not you.

PRAY

God, I am yours and You are mine. Will You teach me the
heights, depths, and lengths of Your love? Will You show
me, tangibly, Your care? I want You, and I know I need You.
Come to my rescue today, so I can be certain of how You
will save me tomorrow. In Jesus's name. Amen.

WRITE THREE THINGS YOU'RE THANKFUL FOR

1. _____

2. _____

3. _____

ENTER YOUR MIND

1. The *Washington Times* reported that, within our mind, we perceive God to be like our earthly father.[2] Consider your father . . .

   What were his best attributes (be specific)?

   His areas of improvement (be specific)?

   How was he there for you or not there (specific examples)?

   How have you ascribed these behaviors to God?

Interestingly, in a recent article I read, I learned that parents who support "autonomy" in children end up with children who believe God is "more forgiving" and "less fearsome."[3]

2. How autonomous did your parents encourage you to be? Where do you see God on the forgiveness scale (1–10)? On the fearful scale (1–10)?

3. Are you afraid of God? Do you fear He'll leave you, abandon you, forsake you, forget you, or no longer want you? Why?

4. How many times have you subconsciously told yourself, *I've got to take care of myself. Everyone hurts me. I will always be hurt* (implying God is not there for you)?

Remember: There is no perfect parent. Forgiveness makes way for peace that makes way for a new move of God's restoration in your heart.

EXAMINE YOUR STORY

1. Write down your "I am" thought patterns you discovered after looking back at your old pictures. Make a list.

2. Identify what kind of stimuli caused you to think these ways. Write them down. What are the patterns?

3. What would a "mind vacation" look like practically in your life? What do you need to stop doing? Start doing? How could you catch yourself when you come down hard?

4. How can you remind yourself to follow through?

EXPLORE WITH GROUP STUDY

This book, in large part, is about finding yourself found in Christ. It's about getting under His love. Not because of your hard-fought effort but because of His effort on the cross. It's about learning to receive, even when you feel breathless and lifeless.

1. Where do you feel breathless and lifeless today? Why?

2. Where do you desire something to come back to life?

3. What do you want found again?

A transformed mind doesn't look like perfection. A transformed mind is one that finds itself under the cross of Jesus Christ time and time again. It is one that is washed, renewed, conformed, and transformed because of His great love. It is one that submits not to feelings but to truth. It is one that accepts His helping hand rather than slapping it away.

4. In what ways have you attempted to slap Christ's hand away in your life? (Every single person should have an answer to this, because we all do it.)

5. Why is it hard for you to receive?

6. What truth can you tell yourself when you're inclined to do this?

7. What might Christ have for you if you stopped doing this?

Everyone who wants Jesus gets Him. If you want Him, seek Him and receive Him—no doubt you'll find Him ever present in your mind. Insecurities don't stand in the way of what God says. Feelings don't block what He's done. Doubt does not hinder reality.

Truth Thoughts

What comes into our minds when we think about God is the most important thing about us.

A. W. Tozer, *The Knowledge of the Holy*

Check these new "I am" statements that most resonate with your heart:

☐ I am part of Christ's royal priesthood.

☐ I am in Him and am not a by-product of people's opinions.

☐ I am beautiful in His eyes.

☐ I am adorned in His righteousness.

☐ I am valuable, seen, and important.

- ☐ I am seated with Christ in the heavenlies.
- ☐ I am His daughter.
- ☐ I am one for whom God goes to great lengths to save.
- ☐ I am shielded by His powerful love, which is my refuge.
- ☐ I am under His fortress of protection.
- ☐ I am made in His image.

Check the "He" statements that revive your soul:

- ☐ He moves obstacles.
- ☐ He rectifies turmoil.
- ☐ He provides what I need, and then some.
- ☐ He cares to know me and be with me.
- ☐ He smiles down on me.
- ☐ He calls me good.
- ☐ He gives me what is best for me.
- ☐ He guards my life.
- ☐ He listens to me.
- ☐ He loves me, not just in word but in deed.

Which of these truths might you need a deeper revelation of? Share with the group.

Now take a moment to pray over each person in your group. Ask God to give you remembrance of His Scripture, love, and sacrifice for that person. Pray with all your heart over their identity, who they are in Christ, and their future. Bless another the way you hope to be blessed.

8. What did God do during this time for you?

Read Luke 15:11–32

9. How are you the prodigal daughter?
10. How is God approaching you right now?

11. What does He do for you in the face of all your mess-ups?
12. How does God's unconditional acceptance of you, back home, change things?

You may need to come home a hundred times while reading this book. Accept that. Then run back into His arms. He waits for you with no condemnation.

To close out the group, take turns going around the circle. Read these verses with your name inserted. Share with the group what God speaks to your heart as you hear Him speaking these words directly to you—about *that* situation.

"____, be still, and know that I am God." (Ps. 46:10)

"____, wait for the LORD; be strong and take heart and wait for the LORD." (Ps. 27:14)

"Call to me, ____, and I will answer you and tell you, ____, great and unsearchable things you do not know." (Jer. 33:3)

A CHRIST-CENTERED PRINCIPLE GOD BLESSES

An identity firmly rooted in the victory of Christ

But you belong to God, my dear children. You have already won a victory over those people, because the Spirit who lives in you is greater than the spirit who lives in the world. (1 John 4:4 NLT)

Warrior Mind-Set Three

She Who Walks with an Open, Receptive Heart Finds It Filled by God

(Sensitivity)

Don't walk in front of me, I may not follow.
Don't walk behind me, I may not lead.
Walk beside me, just be my friend.

Anonymous

Point 1: Want to See God?

Blessed are the pure in heart,
for they *will* see God. (Matt. 5:8)

The word *see* here, based on Strong's Hebrew and Greek definitions, means to:

- Perceive God
- Behold God
- See God
- Discern God Clearly

Could you imagine seeing God unfold this way in your daily life? How the simple sight of Him would change *everything*?

Purity of heart is a high pursuit. The pure in heart get a pure view of God. With this, let's examine three lessons that foster pure hearts.

1. The Drone Lesson

This morning I went on a "mommy/daughter date." We left the house at 5:45 a.m., drove down the quaint roads of downtown Annapolis, Maryland, and headed right to what's called "Ego Alley." Here megaboats sleep along the lengthy inlet, showing off and flexing their horsepower. This particular "date morning" I gripped my three-year-old's hand in one hand and sipped a coffee I held in the other. It was a juggling act for sure as she skipped along, but it didn't matter. I was in my happy place.

She was in hers too. Especially when she stopped to watch a drone fly overhead. She looked at me and said, "Mommy, let's go up to that man with the remote. I want to see what he has."

He overheard her. Holding a massive video screen remote, he made his way over. And showed us—everything. From his view, we could see it all: trees, buildings, people. There was a clarity and crispness from his nearly mile-high view. He could zoom in and zoom out. He could see what I couldn't—expressions on people's faces, the tracks they made, and the details I missed. I asked if he ever spotted and followed specific people. He laughed.

I guess that means yes?

After a while, my dear daughter and I walked away. We grabbed a water at a store, slowly meandered down a few narrow city streets, laughed . . . and then I heard it—*grr . . . grr*. I wasn't sure what animal was tailing us, but then it dropped. His drone. Right before us. I was astonished.

He had us in sight the whole time. He knew every detail of what we did.

I smiled and waved at him; so did my daughter. The mini-plane lifted.

Lesson: God has drone-like vision. He knows exactly where your heart is at. The truth within you, God sees clear as day. He follows along with you because He loves you.

2. *The Snow Pants Lesson*

As a kid, if I wanted to play in the snow, it meant I needed to layer up. I'd pull on long underwear, add shorts, yank up a pair of tights, add more pants, and then . . . ahh . . . I'd finally waddle out into the snow (only to have to go to the bathroom ten minutes later—go figure). I'd sweat the whole way there. Usually, by the time I got outside I was so dense my arms couldn't bend and my legs only spanned half their walking distance (think: Stay Puft Marshmallow Woman). To sit on the sled, I'd plop down backward. The padding barely softened the blow. To get up? I'd get a pull from a friend.

Lesson: Layers never break the hard blows of life; they only make it hard to walk and difficult to get up again and weigh down our hearts.

3. *The Eyeliner Lesson*

To set the stage, God tells us to guard our heart "above all else." It is our most vital organ. "Everything (we) do flows from it" (Prov. 4:23). For instance, if our heart submits to God, leans not on our own instinctual understanding, and trusts God *anyway*, we find straight paths (3:5–6). Yet if we do the opposite—forget God, rely on our mind's understanding, and trust only our wants—our heart likely ventures through rocky terrain.

Choose your own adventure.

REAP > > > SOW > > > SEE

What terrain has your heart been on? Easy roads or tough terrain? Hope or angst? Have you been abiding and thriving or orchestrating and managing everyone and everything?

Thoughts and words are windows to the heart. "A good man brings good things out of the good stored up in his heart, and an evil man brings evil things out of the evil stored up in his heart. For *the mouth speaks what the heart is full of*" (Luke 6:45, emphasis added).

What do your thoughts say? (Check the boxes that apply.)

- ☐ *I don't want to get hurt.*
- ☐ *I must defend myself.*
- ☐ *I can't let that happen again.*
- ☐ *I need to keep safe.*
- ☐ *They'll injure me again.*
- ☐ *I'll look bad.*
- ☐ *I need to hide.*
- ☐ *I'll lay low.*
- ☐ *I must be seen as better than I am.*
- ☐ *I can't be open, honest, or authentic anymore.*
- ☐ *I can't really be me. They'll judge me.*

Is your heart receptive or deflective? Search deep. Then go deeper by considering your protective layers. Do you ever think:

- ☐ *I am okay to act this way because . . . This is* **rationalization**.
- ☐ *I don't have a problem.* This is **denial**.
- ☐ *He has the issue . . . he is always . . .* This is **projection**.
- ☐ *I need to release tension.* You get furious. This is **explosion**.
- ☐ *I am 100 percent A-okay, and no, nothing is at all wrong with me.* This is **pretending**.
- ☐ *I can fend off the issue by pushing away my feelings. It's not that big of a deal, anyway.* This is **negating**.

☐ *I am so angry at him, just furious.* You then kick the front door—hard—or you take it out on your kids. This is **replacement**.

☐ *I am embarrassed, unsure, or caught, but oh . . . looky here . . . this is a nice shirt I can buy online . . . or wait, should I buy that one?* This is **distraction** (and includes humor, sarcasm, or attention shifting).

☐ *I shouldn't have done that. I'll just pour out praise, good words, and acclaim on the person. Maybe they won't notice.* This is **fixing**.

☐ *I'll use humor, sarcasm, or an insult, so I don't have to deal with this.* This is **diversion**.

☐ *I can't change because . . .* This is **a lie**.[1]

Ignoring the pain doesn't negate the problem. Friends, a cavity is still a cavity even if we pretend it's not there. We may ignore the hurt, but the pain eventually becomes excruciating. The hard truth is denial can't deny away the truth of a hurting heart before a seeing God.

I understand, many of us have questions or situations that feel too hard to confront. We don't know how to fix, manage, or tie up the loose ends. We don't know how to come to terms with the reality. We don't know how to deal with the pain, the embarrassment, the weak-kneed feelings of it all, or the hard memories. I get all this.

But if God remains God, do we really have to know? Doesn't God know? Doesn't He already have a high-level view of our exact way?

Perhaps healing is as simple as us asking:

Do You think I am bad, God? Are You angry with me?

What is the worst-case scenario of me seeing my weakness? Of me changing?

God, how do I handle this?

God, will You really take care of me if I am honest? If I am vulnerable?

God, will You abandon me because I am not perfect?

How can I really confront what I am afraid to see, God, without it killing me?

What is the worst-case scenario of me approaching this in a different way?

What truths repair the hurt that exist in me?

Look into the eyes of your heart. I do this when I put on eyeliner. As I circle my eyes with the charcoal color, I look for *my* deep. In me, I try to examine and search for the true condition of my heart.

In the deep of my being, while staring into the eye of who I am, I wonder, *Where am I really at? Am I happy? Am I struggling? Look how much I've gone through.* I choose to see the real me.

Likewise, look into your own eyes, examine deeply, and ask: *What protective layers do I need to confront? Am I being honest with my God who sees me and wants to love me?*

Then, go deeper. Ask yourself why. *Why am I doing these things? Why am I believing they work? Why do I need to do this? How have these techniques really helped me? How do they keep me lonely and isolated?*

Get real, get on a mind vacation, and get your heart opened right up to the God who desires to repair it.

Lesson: When we forgo self-protection and move into prayerful introspection we find deep connection with God. We actually come to see God at work in us.

Points to remember:

God already sees where your heart is at.

Layers don't help but rather hurt you.

Self-protection is a waste, but through prayerful introspection, you see God.

**Point 2: Ten-Second Techniques to Leverage the Power
of Your Mini-Mind**

I am intrigued with Amazon.com. Truly. If we buy something,
Amazon knows what else we should be buying. The exact batteries
we'll need with that toy. The proper mattress to go with the bed
frame. The books we'll like because we liked this one.

Amazon gets a step ahead of our mind. Likewise, our heart is
often a step ahead of our brain. In fact, some scientists call our
heart our "heart brain." Here, forty thousand neurons fire off to
help us to feel, sense, process, remember, decide, and learn. Within
this organ, a neurotransmitter called oxytocin induces love. Even
more, according to Heartmath.org, "the heart actually sends more
signals to the brain than the brain sends to the heart."[2]

Imagine that. To mind our mind effectively we must truly mind
our mini-mind.

This little lever can shift our whole life.

God knows it. I believe this is why the word *heart* is written
nearly three hundred times in the Bible. It stands out like a big ol'
Attention! sign. Our heart is our health.

> Above all else, guard your heart, for everything you do flows from
> it. (Prov. 4:23)

> As he thinketh in his heart, so is he. (Prov. 23:7 KJV)

Your heart is the head of your life. Your mini-mind rules. We
must mind our mini-mind too in order to mind our mind.

Let's think deeper about this for a moment. If your heart says,
*I've been stuck without a friend or spouse for years and people
don't like me*, it tells your mind things like: *You must protect
yourself from getting hurt. Expect what has happened to happen
again. Be cautious about people.*

Or, if your heart says, *I am always abandoned and I always
will be*, your hurt heart tells your mind: *Avoid people, at all costs.*

Hurt people first so you don't get hurt. Only partially invest in relationships.

Your heart talks to your mind, which acts. For instance, your heart tells your mind, *You're hurt*, so you unload hurtful words onto others. Your heart tells your mind, *You're embarrassing*, so you shrink back, ashamed of what you don't do. Your heart tells your mind, *Your husband is forgetting you*, so you explode when he leaves the toilet seat up.

HEART > > > MIND > > > ACTION (SEE)

The mind often follows the impulses of the heart. This is why we must take a full-hearted approach to minding our thoughts. We don't want to work hard only to end up brokenhearted. The heart is the hearth to all we think, do, and say.

Jesus knew this. He addressed people's hearts first. In Bethesda, which translates to "House of Mercy," people gathered at a pool of water. The sick came, hoping to be made well. One man in particular was "an invalid for thirty-eight years" (John 5:5).

Jesus didn't just outright approach this man and heal him.

Or, from afar, declare him "healed through the name of Jesus."

Or lift the man high and say, "Today you'll be healed." He did none of this.

When Jesus saw him lying there, he said, "Do you want to get well?" (v. 6).

I believe Jesus asks us the same question.

Do you really want to get well?

Do you really want to be healed of your fear, your complacency, your bad attitudes, or your worry to find a free-flying, abounding life? You know you'll have to radically change things.

Or are you used to things as they are? Are you accustomed to the sympathies, the comforts, the leniencies, the excuses, and the status of *poor old me*?

Do you want this new thing?

I believe Jesus asks, "[Insert your name], you say you want this, but do you really want radical passion and purpose? Or, has your heart settled into complacent and comfortable patterned living?"

God is a giver, but He doesn't force the best of Himself on those fully satisfied with lesser gods or lesser goals.

Are you ready to get well?

Now, if your heart isn't ready to move, I caution you about reading on. If your heart won't move, neither will your mind nor your life.

But if your heart is even the slightest bit ready for a new beginning, these are some of the exact things you should consider doing:

1. Take an inventory of where you pretend and are fake in life. Seek God's authentic way. Make an agreement with Him to be honest.

2. Confess what guilt (sin) you know to be on your heart. Ask God to show you what you cannot see. Ask Him to grant you the grace to chart a new path and to deliver you from temptation (which He will).

3. Abstain from a mentality that is always offended. Forgive others.

4. Show shame the light of Jesus's empty tomb so His truth can flood it.

5. Write a list of both regrets and fears. Acknowledge how they've restricted you in life.

6. Release bitterness to make room for godly progress in your heart.

7. Shut off any and all distractions that take your attention from points 1–6 above. Remember: your heart is your health.

The best heart-procedure is to say, like David, "Search me, God, and know my heart; test me and know my anxious thoughts" (Ps. 139:23).

Then wait. Be prepared to act differently. Become a woman "after God's own heart."

Then you'll find:

1. Peace.
2. God's unwavering will.
3. That your problem isn't the problem. Your doubting vision is the problem.
4. Unwavering heart confidence.
5. Strength because of His faithfulness.

A strong dependence on God mentally beats your loud-speaking, always-shifting feelings.

Speaking of Feelings: We Need to Know

FEELINGS ≠ TRUTH
FEELINGS = RANDOM REACTIONS
DRIVING US TO IMPULSIVE ACTIONS

Has your mouth ever gotten ahead of your mind, getting you in trouble? Have you ever thought something was true of someone, only to find out it was not? Have you ever completely misunderstood a situation only to wish for a rewind?

Our untested feelings often create unsavory predicaments. Just think: our sadness builds on our sadness until we land in a depression hole. Our pent-up anger builds and builds until we throw something across the room. Our annoyance severs a good friendship.

SOW A FEELING > > >
REAP A RESPONSE > > >
SEE IT PLAY OUT IN YOUR LIFE

"Hope deferred makes the heart sick" (Prov. 13:12).

Sow hopelessness. Reap discouragement. See sickness. Our mind problems translate to life problems.

We lack hope. We can't get out of bed, or pick up a phone to call a friend, or take a walk in the summer air, or get our mind on anyone else beside ourselves, or think good thoughts about people. We get sick with depression, loneliness, isolation, and fear.

See the heart of the matter?

But what if we used our heart-brained mini-mind to our advantage? What if we learned to make good decisions rather than impulsive, unreliable ones? We can. We can leverage our emotions to our advantage. How? By exchanging our "always have" responses for "now can" redirects.

Let me explain.

Example 1

"Always have" response: "I always have felt overwhelming anger, worry, and frustration at news stations that speak against my political views."

"Always have" feeling/habit: judgment and disappointment.

"Now can" redirect: (This includes not only a new way to act but a consideration of a new feeling after you do it. For instance, "By removing judgment, guilt, and disappointment, I can feel more love.")

1. Imagine what peace might feel like if you turned off the TV. Imagine the heart-healthy things you could do that still might move the dial in the world.

   Invoke: peace

2. Consider the joy that could be felt if you called that one friend. Remember how you always laugh together when you're on the phone. Feel excited. Call her.

   Invoke: joy

3. Ask yourself what you get from the news. Perhaps it is a sense you are doing something to change the world. Stop watching and instead take action. Go do something to change the world.

   Invoke: love

Example 2

"Always have" response: "I always have mean thoughts about my husband or a loved one; I silently critique them."

"Always have" feeling/habit: criticism.

"Now can" redirect:

1. Look for the good. Rather than seeing your husband's mess on the bathroom floor as a personal assault, see it as a blessing: he is still physically well and alive.

   Invoke: appreciation

2. Tell God so-and-so really keeps you learning and growing. Marvel at the things you are learning from a positive perspective (patience, kindness, grace, etc.).

   Invoke: awe

3. Ask yourself what feeling you receive by criticizing. (Example: perhaps it is a sense you are better off than they are. Pride.) Instead, search out their good; look for what is awesome about them.

   Invoke: humility

Example 3

"Always have" response: when you go on Facebook, you scroll to see your wrinkle-free friend beachside in St. Lucia, your quasi-friends meeting up for a twinkle-light dinner, or your smart friend graduating from medical school.

"Always have" feeling/habit: jealousy.

"Now can" redirect:

1. Remember far-off friends and all the fun times you had together. Relive those. Write them a postcard. Let them know how much you care.

   Invoke: belonging and love

2. Consider there are two sides to every story. The one on vacation may be trying to rekindle a marriage that is on the verge of divorce.

   Invoke: sympathy

3. Ask yourself what you get from Facebook. A sense that you are better or worse off than someone else? Rather than looking for worth from others, choose to bless them. Pray for them, write to them, connect.

   Invoke: care and the joy of walking like Christ

We can harness our emotions to make good habits stick.

A General Framework to Make New Habits Work

1. Observe the bad habit.
2. Note the emotion that tends to "flick you" or "tick you off." Hint: it's the thing that "always gets you" (example: when people are better than you, when you feel ugly, when someone acts smarter than you). Acknowledge the feeling (jealousy, comparison, etc.).
3. Apply the "always have/now can" approach. Remember, entice your heart with the new feel-good emotion or the blessing that will result by doing it (see examples above).

4. Imagine the freedom, the peace, the new space to walk with God, the hope, the friendships . . . all the good that will come because of your new action.

5. Take a mind vacation if you mess up. Then return to this process each time you encounter the issue. By doing this, you create new neural pathways or tracks in your mind. These will become go-to, default responses over time.

"Do you want to get well?" After the man admitted his need, Jesus told the invalid, "Get up! Pick up your mat and walk" (John 5:8). He was healed.

Want to be well? Admit your real heartfelt, vulnerable, delayered need. Get up. Pick up your mat and walk.

Point 3: Get Your Heart-Health Checkup

A mom passed me a note. Apparently, her kid wanted to play with my kid. I told my three-year-old daughter, "So-and-so wants to play with you."

Madison screamed loudly and repeatedly for what seemed like a good five minutes, "No . . . ooo . . . ooo! Anyone but *her*!"

Some of us need to protest, like Madison, "No . . . ooo . . . ooo, anything but *that*!"

We need to throw a fit about what we see in our heart, saying, "Noo . . . ooo . . . not that!" What do you see in there?

Here are some questions to help you search your heart.

• Do TV, news, social media, gossip articles, text messages, emails, or videos seem to leave you tense, worried, or feeling unpure?

• Do you find yourself running so much you can't sit with God?

• Do you, like Jesus did (ahem . . . Judas), have an idea of the people likely to betray you? Do you keep a healthy heart distance from them?

- Do you safeguard important relationships? For example, do you put boundaries around your marriage?
- Do you protect prayer time as if it is your first line of defense?
- Do you focus on what people want of you (Pinterest party, a clean house, good behavior, good church attendance, award-winning service, law keeping, etc.), or do you focus on how God loves being with you?
- Do you consider all that will undoubtedly go wrong, or do you consider a good God is working out good for you, right here, right now, because you love Him (Rom. 8:28)?
- Do you just exist with your body, or do you take care of it by feeding it right and taking it on a walk?
- Do you memorize the Word of God and store it in you for hard times, or do you brush past it, moving quickly to the next thing?
- Do you notice what people, things, or circumstances irritate you, frustrate you, or cause you to sin? Do you make changes as you are able (think of your approach, timing, avoidance, wisdom, softened words, etc.), or do you continue to hit your head against the window like an oblivious fly?
- Do you guard your eyes, ears, and body from defiling your heart? Or do you let all things in?
- Do you immediately ask for forgiveness and accept God's grace? Or do you criticize, condemn, and never allow God to forgive you?
- Do you quickly react to worldly pursuits (the inclination to feel jealous or compare), or do you let spiritual ones define you first?
- Do you obey God's truth and guidance, or do you constantly question if you heard Him right?
- Do you act resentfully toward yourself and others? Or do you love with no strings attached?

Take Heart Key

You can choose to take heart by remembering:

[Jesus has] overcome the world. (John 16:33)

[God] will sustain me to the end, so I'll be blameless on the day of my Lord Jesus Christ. (1 Cor. 1:8)

God is able to keep me from stumbling [into sin] and to present me before His glorious presence without fault and with great joy. (Jude 24)

I can do all things through God who gives me strength. (Phil. 4:13)

It is written: "What no eye has seen, what no ear has heard, and what no human mind has conceived"—the things God has prepared for those who love Him. (1 Cor. 2:9)

[Nothing] will be able to separate [me] from the love of God that is in Christ Jesus our Lord. (Rom. 8:39)

- Do you notice what God is doing or speaking to you in His Word and bend toward it, or are you inflexible, finding it hard to change?

What did you learn about yourself? What do you need to change? Note it, but take on no shame. This is a shame-free zone. The perfect One died and rose again so you don't have to die trying to be perfect. Jesus can handle your weakness. He sympathizes with it (Heb. 4:15) and works with it as you bring it to Him. In fact, His power is made perfect within your weakness.

He who began a good work in you will carry it on to completion until the day of Christ Jesus. (Phil. 1:6)

[Jesus's] power is made perfect in weakness. (2 Cor. 12:9)

Point 4: Ten Proven Strategies to Cultivate a Big Heart

This is important: a big, healthy, godly heart doesn't look like a perfect heart.

We often mistake this point. This is why we have to keep on establishing it, and then reestablishing it three days later. It's open hearts, not perfect hearts, that find the grace of God that lets them stay near Him. They know how to "return" well. They come back, turn around, and head home to God—often. They keep on. They remain open to God's leading and transforming.

These people live a repentance lifestyle. Like living a healthy lifestyle or an active lifestyle or a family lifestyle, a repentance lifestyle is a way of life. If you live a lifestyle, you're sold out to it. It is almost your being.

Repentance means, in Greek, "to change one's mind," to literally turn your feet around. It means you're humble enough to see: (1) you were wrong; (2) God is right; (3) a course change is needed; and (4) God has something better for you on that other course.

A repentance lifestyle lives by humility and a softened heart. This is an all-the-time deal. It's not something you do once a month but is an every-second posture. It is to be fully aware of where God is and to analyze if you are *with* Him or away. This is a repentance lifestyle.

Strong women live this way. They don't fear repentance means retaliation by God; they know it is restoration. An interior make-over in the best possible way.

Jesus "heals the brokenhearted and binds up their wounds" (Ps. 147:3). Notice He doesn't shame them for being broken and send them away without dinner. He doesn't rip off their clothes and point at their indiscretions. He repairs and restores them to purity. He makes them pure.

"Blessed are the pure in heart, for they will see God" (Matt. 5:8).

Pure people see God and see everything their heart could ever desire.

God fills them better than a piece of chocolate, makes them look better than a facial, embraces them more than a new husband ever could, and gives them more joy than could be packaged up in a new house or clothes. God is the fulfillment of all our heart has ever craved. Pure people see God.

How? How do we start to see God more?

1. We Keep a Clay-Soft Heart

Clay is movable. It can be fashioned into the image of Jesus. Even if it's heard the whole Bible five hundred times, it doesn't pretend to know it all or have it all down pat. It considers and reconsiders. It surrenders. It asks God to reveal its real nature. It understands it is the creation, not the Creator.

> Yet you, LORD, are our Father. We are the clay, you are the potter; we are all the work of your hand. (Isa. 64:8)

HOW TO:

- Lay down or kneel before God. Take your heart out of its box; let the walls fall. Acknowledge the power, control, and might of God.
- Take notice of what God is calling you to change, reconsider, or bring before Him. Don't hide your feelings but let them stand before His throne so He can reform them.
- Remember: God is not a human that He will see your bad attitude and hate you. On the contrary, He will heal you as you are transparent with Him.

2. We Delight

We dance with God. Smile at Him. Consider Him visible through our day. Sing to Him. Perform before Him. Pour out love on others in such a way we're almost sure He's smiling. Accept His already-given peace. Let in His joy. Stop along the way to talk to Him. Filter the choices and voices we let in.

Delight yourself in the LORD, and he will give you the desires of your heart. (Ps. 37:4 ESV)

HOW TO:

- Pick a name of God (for example: Lion, Lamb, or Prince of Peace). Notice how God shows up in your life that way. Praise and thank Him for His care.

Therefore, as you received Christ Jesus the Lord, so walk in him, rooted and built up in him and established in the faith, just as you were taught, abounding in thanksgiving. (Col. 2:6–7 ESV)

- Use *and* and *because*. Add the word *and* at the end of every negative statement you say. (Example: "This situation is horrible *and* God is going to bring me through it.") Take it a step further with the word *because*. (Example: "This situation is horrible *and* God is going to bring me through it *because* He is faithful, always.")
- Write a letter to God. In the letter, praise God for who He is, how He comes through, what He does, and all the ways He shows up. Be specific. Remember what He has done for you. Encourage yourself by remembering the unchanging nature of God. Allow His joy to be full in you.
- Read the Bible for who God *is*. Understand His character.

3. We Make Heart Care a Priority

Then, because so many people were coming and going that [the disciples] did not even have a chance to eat, [Jesus] said to them, "Come with me by yourselves to a quiet place and get some rest." (Mark 6:31)

HOW TO:

- Take a break. A break is a time-out, a pulling away, and a stepping aside from it all.
- Do something that brings you soul replenishment (take a walk, do a craft, draw a picture, read and pause with God, etc.).

Reroute your mind with a morning routine.

 Wake.

 Thank God you are alive.

 Ask to meet God through your day.

 Listen to praise music as you get dressed.

 Imagine the Word of God coming to life as a story, as you read it.

 Pick a verse to hold near as you go through your day.

- Notice your heart. Notice where peace is. Notice where peace isn't. Pursue peace.
- Think back to what thrills you. (This is not what people think you are good at, this is what your heart loves to do.)
- Give room to ponder God's heart, voice, and truth.
- Accept His heart prompts that lead to love.
- Take the risk to participate with God in profound and unusual ways.

4. We Keep Sacred Time

It is in the unseen that we cultivate what is seen. It takes God's inner working to grow outer strength.

> But when you pray, go into your room and shut the door and pray to your Father who is in secret. And your Father who sees in secret will reward you. (Matt. 6:6 ESV)

HOW TO:

- Cry out to God in the quiet.
- Every time your mind wants to stray, return it to when you were last considering God. Start up again with that thought, not with self-condemnation. Keep doing this until your mind learns to stay connected.
- See prayer time as your battleground, where wars are lost or won.

5. We Admit Need

In my distress I called to the LORD; I cried to my God for help. From his temple he heard my voice; my cry came before him, into his ears. (Ps. 18:6)

HOW TO:

- Notice what you utter under your breath at people or circumstances. Ask God for clarity on why these things upset you.

- Remember the drone and the fact that you are not left alone. When you cry to Him, expect God's response. Listen for His still, small voice; discern His leading through people; and pray for confirmation in your life. Submit everything under the authority of His Word.
- Reflect on the truth you don't suffer alone. There are many trying to go through a day without crying. Look out for these people in your life. Pray for them too. Unite and share your struggle.
- Consider how God loves you: "You have collected all my tears in your bottle. You have recorded each one in your book" (Ps. 56:8).

6. We Are Accountable

Seek accountability and have a plan.

Therefore, confess your sins to one another and pray for one another, that you may be healed. The prayer of a righteous person has great power as it is working. (James 5:16 ESV)

HOW TO:
- Schedule a set time to pray together.
- Prepare to be delayered and vulnerable. Consider your deep and real struggle.
- Listen well to the other person, without advice. Then pray.
- Don't let offenses get in the way. Honestly share any hurts that arise between you.
- Ask the Holy Spirit to show you how to best love the other person.

7. We Are a Storehouse

I have stored up your word in my heart, that I might not sin against you. (Ps. 119:11 ESV)

HOW TO:

- Write three verses on notecards and leave them around your house. Change their locations on a regular basis.
- Pick a morning verse and repeat it and own it through your day. The more you say it, the more you will remember it.
- Ask God to reveal His heart to you as you say it aloud. Expect Him to reveal astonishing things.

8. We Apply a Two-Second Time-Out

Everyone should be quick to listen, slow to speak and slow to become angry. (James 1:19)

HOW TO:

- When you feel your temperature rising, give your mind and heart a two-second time-out before responding to people. In this time, consider, "How would Love talk?"
- If you still can't speak in love, don't speak. Only speak what communicates life. It is not what we don't say that hurts people, but what we do. Silence is a holy calling.
- Processing with God is wisdom. Asking for His words to speak is brilliance.

9. We Gush from the Heart

Love the LORD your God with all your heart and with all your soul and with all your strength. (Deut. 6:5)

HOW TO:

- Pick an attribute of God (faith, truth, love, peace, etc.). Choose to see this attribute in your day. Notice how God is that way to you, to others, to nature, to the earth, to humankind.
- Worship, praise, and marvel at God's greatness in your past, present, and future-to-come.

- Acknowledge God is triumphant over trials. Envision His glory. His strength. His power. His might. His love at work on your behalf. Dwell on His goodness to come, not your pain in a present moment.

10. We Are Imaginative

Jesus used parables to help people imagine what His point was. Bible-centered imagination paints a picture of something new. It shows you the potential of what could be. Don't fear it; use it for godly growth.

HOW TO:

- Use your "heart brain." Imagine how you will feel as a result of kicking a heart-hurting habit to the curb. Use the blessings of God's fruit of the Spirit (Gal. 5:22–23) as an incentive to act differently. And please note: even more than what you've imagined, God can do.
- Imagine God smiling down on you as you trust Him with the scary things of your day. See yourself leaning on Him when you feel you can't stand. Praise His name and feel Him smiling back at you through your suffering.
- Imagine who God has created you to be and what He has created you to do. Imagine how you feel as you let go of all that has held you back.

When you set up God to rule over your life: no doubt, your heart can't help but rule over your head.

Point 5: What's So Great about BIG Open Hearts

Like a clean house seems to give us permission to have friends over, a clean heart makes inviting God in easier.

We want God in, I assure you. Because when He comes, He

- plants us by streams of water so we bear fruit. Our leaves don't wither and *whatever we do* prospers (Ps. 1:3).
- watches over us, the righteous (Ps. 1:6).
- works all things together for our good (Rom. 8:28).
- gives us unfading beauty in His eyes (1 Pet. 3:3–4).
- makes our life reflect the goodness of our heart (Ps. 27:19).
- offers us favor and a good name in the sight of God and other people (Prov. 3:3–4).
- allows us to "see" Himself (Matt. 5:8).
- gives us the desires of our heart (Ps. 37:4).
- brings peace and prosperity (Prov. 3:1–2).
- leads us to joy in His statutes (Ps. 119:111).
- blesses us (Ps. 119:1).
- delivers us to a full and happy life (Ps. 119:45).
- makes life long (Prov. 3:2).
- guides us and lights up our path (Ps. 119:105).
- offers wisdom (Eccles. 2:26).
- helps us understand we really are a city on a hill (Matt. 5:14).
- reveals Himself to others (Ezek. 38:23).

To have God "in" is to never want to be outside His love.

"For the LORD God is a sun and shield; the LORD bestows favor and honor; no good thing does he withhold from those whose walk is blameless" (Ps. 84:11). Full of God, our heart becomes fully loaded with every good thing we need to fight our fight.

<<< DOWNLOAD >>> "6 Heart-Steadying Morning Prayers To Help You Take Heart" at www.iambattleready.com.

Remember:
—THE DRONE
—THE SNOW PANTS
—THE EYELINER

※

Search YOUR HEART
AND TAKE HEART

※

Live A REPENTANCE LIFESTYLE

※

Keep THE HOUSE CLEAN

※

To Have GOD "IN" IS TO
NEVER WANT HIM TO LEAVE

A MIND TO CONQUER

It's always a matter of the heart.

PRAY

Father, I have little idea of what is going on in my heart. I confess, I don't pay that much attention to it. I don't really consider it. Will You show me what You see? Will You lead me to grasp Your purity? Will You hold my hand through the process and make known what You want to? I trust You. I am expectant of the new things You will do. Thank You, God. In Jesus's name. Amen.

WRITE THREE THINGS YOU'RE THANKFUL FOR

1. _____

2. _____

3. _____

ENTER YOUR MIND

Are you afraid to make mistakes? Do you quickly shun them away? Or do you harness them to learn from them?

> New neuropsychological research is now suggesting that the inability to learn from one's mistakes may indeed be at the root of a broad range of human problems, ranging from childhood bullying and truancy to aggressive acts like road rage to all manner of substance abuse. And this cognitive aberration, deep-wired into the neurons and genes, may even underlie the vagaries of normal human behavior and personality.[3]

89

EXAMINE YOUR STORY

1. Prepare your heart. Pray this over yourself (add to it, put your story into it, and insert your name or your heart within these words):

> Cleanse me with hyssop, and I will be clean;
>> wash me, and I will be whiter than snow.
> Let me hear joy and gladness;
>> let the bones you have crushed rejoice.
> Hide your face from my sins
>> and blot out all my iniquity.
> Create in me a pure heart, O God,
>> and renew a steadfast spirit within me.
> Do not cast me from your presence
>> or take your Holy Spirit from me.
> Restore to me the joy of your salvation
>> and grant me a willing spirit, to sustain me. (Ps. 51:7–12)

2. In what ways do you defend yourself (excuses, rationalization, etc.)?

3. How has this played out in relationships? How has it hurt them?

4. How has truth felt like something that was impossible for you? (Be specific and detailed.)

5. What does this chapter teach you about truth?

6. How is God calling you to soften your heart to His work? What would this look like in your daily life?

7. Write out five "always have" thought processes and some "now can" redirects.

_____

_____

_____

EXPLORE WITH GROUP STUDY

1. What did you learn from your personal study time?
2. Repentance isn't retaliation by God; it is restoration by Him. In what ways has repentance felt more like punishment than purity? More like fear than hope? More like agony than restoration? How does God's love change the fear you feel when you mess up?
3. What would you have to change in your life to live a repentance lifestyle? Let go of? Add?
4. In what ways do you need to "take heart"?
5. "Those who live in accordance with the Spirit have their minds set on what the Spirit desires" (Rom. 8:5). What did you find when you "searched your heart"? What does this verse mean for your heart? How can you set your heart on these things? What boundaries might you need to set up?

A CHRIST-CENTERED PRINCIPLE
GOD BLESSES

Sensitivity of heart

Create in me a clean heart, O God, and renew a right spirit within me. (Ps. 51:10 ESV)

Intermission One

A Minding Grace Note

Dear Reader,

If you're like me, right now you may believe you've got a whole lot to do, change, and improve upon. You, perhaps, feel caught up in . . . all you are not. Friends, may I encourage you: if Jesus is your Lord and Savior, you already have the mind of Christ. A mind of freedom. You are His new creation. With this, it is not striving that will progress you forward but rather abiding, sitting with God, and following His heart prompts. You have permission to rest in Jesus. Breathe deep. He has afforded you the grace you need to lie down in His care. Jesus will faithfully be your guide. You are under His supernatural care.

Love,
Kelly

I became a servant of this gospel by the gift of God's grace given me through the working of his power. (Eph. 3:7)

Warrior Mind-Set Four

The Difference between Complacency and Victory Is Action

(Activity)

Love is never stationary.

Bob Goff, *Love Does*

Point 1: The Awe-Inspiring Art of *Just Do It*

I recently read about Maria Spelterini, a twenty-three-year-old woman unafraid of her unique abilities. In 1876, this woman walked a tightrope across the rushing massiveness of Niagara Falls in a pretty dress. The fun didn't stop there. Time and time again she did new things. She went across blindfolded, dressed up, with peach baskets on her feet, or with her hands tied. She was quite the spectacle.[1]

When I think of Maria, I can almost hear the ladies whispering. "Who does she think she is?" "Did you see what she wore?" "How dare she try something like that?" "No woman can do that!"

Maria went for it.

Sure, Maria could have thought, *I'll look dumb. People will talk about me. I could fail.* But, she didn't let her idiosyncrasies, her uniqueness, her oddness stop her. She didn't let outside voices hold her back.

Instead, Maria put one foot in front of the other and she kept going, little by little, until she arrived at the other side.

Until the *impossible*—crossing over Niagara Falls on a tightrope, blindfolded—became *possible.*

There was almost certainly one day, before her grand accomplishment, she just started. Where she got up from daydreaming, put on her shoes, stepped into her backyard, assembled a tightrope, and just . . . did it. A day where she gave it a shot, even if she was only a foot above the ground.

So what?

The act of trying is a setup for the miraculous.

Where is God calling you to try? To trust Him, to make a change, to grab hold of a dream, or to treat someone differently? What might you need to press into even if it appears laughable, impossible, beyond your ability, or nearly idiotic?

Move on it. And don't get caught up in the awkwardness of it. New things, like new jeans, take time to fit like a glove. Embrace the oddness, the feeling you're a little "out of your mind" for trying. You know, people thought Jesus was out of His mind. That never stopped Him.

> They said, "[Jesus] is *out of his mind.*" And the teachers of the law who came down from Jerusalem said, "He is possessed by Beelzebul! By the prince of demons he is driving out demons." (Mark 3:21–22, emphasis added)

People talk. There will always be vocal dream-killers and shame-speakers. They walk all around us. They speak opposition and unknowingly try to hold us back while gut-wrenchingly laughing at our dreams. They point fingers. What does it matter what they do?

We don't serve them. We serve God. The one who does not limit us but unlimits us by His grace. Go by His Word, not theirs. Who cares if you appear an "extremist" of love? Who cares if they call you "out of your mind"? The day generosity, kindness, and forgiveness have madly multiplied within you is a good day, I assure you.

Circle back to this truth.

Choose decisively to move out on wild, nearly scandalous faith. Scandalous faith pushes love forward even when there's no evidence, proof, or good reason to do so. Faith knows God has good reason. By faith, creativity, restoration, progress, life, music, messages, business acumen, wisdom, skill, and wonder are released, all to the stand-back glory of God. Stagnation is dead faith.

Where do you fall on the spectrum? Faith-full or faith-becoming?

Set up your tightrope. Even if it's just a millimeter above ground. Just do it. Try, even if people talk, even if you are pointed out as the village idiot.

> Am I now trying to win the approval of human beings, or of God? Or am I trying to please people? If I were still trying to please people, I would not be a servant of Christ. (Gal. 1:10)

Spirit-filled, empowered women step out despite

opinions,

risks,

failure,

their past track record, or

their perception of themselves.

How can you prepare your mind to follow through, despite these things? What can you tell yourself? (Example: "[God] is able to do immeasurably more than all we ask or imagine, according to his power that is at work within us" [Eph. 3:20].) Write down your motivational truths. Refer to them.

Prepare your mind with new thoughts so you don't end up shrinking back, saying *I'll look dumb; I'll be a laughingstock; they'll think I am weird; I'll be judged; they'll make fun of me; I'll feel bad; it will feel too hard . . . [fill in the blank] . . .*

Or don't.

And let people, opinions, and fears keep you exactly where you are today.

⚜

Charles Blondin was a classic "just do it" man. He also tightroped across Niagara Falls, but he did it in a sack, on stilts, with a bike, carrying a stove, and even cooking up some omelets along the way. People loved, cheered, and believed in him. His risk kept becoming success.

So one day, Charles turned toward his fans and said, "Do you believe I can carry a person across in this wheelbarrow?"

The crowds roared, "Yes!" They believed. But guess who wanted to take the ride in the wheelbarrow across with him? No one.

Their emotions said, "Yes, he can do it!" Their mind said, "No way, José! I don't believe *that* much."

We often don't believe *that much* either. We sing songs that say we do and confess words that sound nice, but when push comes to shove, we don't. So we stay stuck halfway, treading water, sinking, and getting nowhere.

We fail to move decisively or to even try.

So we don't get off our La-Z-Boy recliners or our big ol' couch. We don't hop up or pull on our frilly dress or grab hold of our mini-bag of teensy-weensy belief. We don't just do it. Instead, we believe we *can't* and we hate everyone else who does something. We critique the pants off of successful women doing their own tightrope walk. We deem their rope "easy." We internally chastise God for not making us like them and for giving us "unreachable dreams." We go to church on Sunday.

We do nothing and hate everyone.

We grow cynical and hate life. *Blah*.

You know, things could be different. Right here, right now, we could change the course of our life, by simply deciding to *just do it*.

Point 2: Six Beliefs That Compound Complacency

Ever dreamed of being superwoman? Changing the world? Leaving a legacy of change? Feeling meaningful? Adding value? Helping the needy? In our own way, we are all invited to a life of impact.

> He sent his servants to those who had been invited to the banquet to tell them to come, but they refused to come. . . . Then he sent some more servants and said, "Tell those who have been invited that I have prepared my dinner." . . . But *they paid no attention* and went off—one to his field, another to his business. (Matt. 22:3–6, emphasis added)

What invitation is God extending you? Are you paying attention? Or are you heading off to life-and-thoughts as usual?

God doesn't always bow down to meet us in our predictable, comfortable lifestyle. Often He calls us into the unpredictable so we can find an unbelievable new road.

Yet to find this adventure, to just do it, we are wise to examine the thought patterns that bind us to our couch, make us feel shame, and keep us operating within a life of predictability.

These six thoughts compound complacency:

1. *God better show up. He better move me to where I want to be (just like I expect, like I want him to, etc.).*

    Want God only your way? Can't adapt to change? There is almost no worse feeling than demanding to be where God isn't calling you.

See, I am doing a new thing! Now it springs up; do you not perceive it? I am making a way in the wilderness and streams in the wasteland. (Isa. 43:19)

2. *I don't believe in God enough, so everything I do is bound to fail, not work, or not be blessed.*

Jesus's name is Faithful and True. Sometimes getting back to faith is as simple as saying, "My body feels weak and my emotions feel wounded. But it is not about me; it is all about God. And my God is as faithful as ever. . . . He will do it!"

If we are faithless, he remains faithful—for he cannot deny himself. (2 Tim. 2:13 ESV)

3. *I need to do this whole "Christian thing" better. I need to be perfect. I can't make a mistake.*

There is no perfect Christian. There also is no use in demanding yourself do better. It's like scratching a mosquito bite and thinking it'll help. It doesn't. It only aggravates things even more. Let go of your hard-driving demands and find God's soft hand ready to help you.

For it is by grace you have been saved, through faith—and this is not from yourselves, it is the gift of God—not by works, so that no one can boast. (Eph. 2:8–9)

4. *I don't know what to do or how to do it.*

Sometimes I think, *If Jesus would just come and be clear, I'd listen. But Jesus ain't speaking and I'm stuck.*

Zacchaeus, a short man, must have understood this thinking. He couldn't see Jesus. He couldn't see over the crowds; he was blocked.

This didn't stop him. Looking "out of his mind," he climbed a tree. Leaving all else behind, he moved his mind to the places where he could see God.

We must do the same. We must lift our mind to God's height. We do this by saying:

"God, You are above my need to have money to put dinner on the table."

"God, You have control of all the details of this argument with my sister."

"God, help me see how to love her through Your eyes."

"God, what is Your humble view of how I can work all I have to do today?"

"God, You have all authority over my health."

Seek Jesus and you'll find Him working, intimately, right where you are.

> [Jesus] looked up and said to him, "Zacchaeus, come down immediately. I must stay at your house today." (Luke 19:5)

5. *My way looks "dumb," "not as good," and "clearly second-rate."*

The first time I read Maria Spelterini's story, I halfway read it and played it out in my head to end like this: "Maria Spelterini put on a fancy and frilly outfit only to cross the Niagara Falls tightrope and fall to her demise. The applause of man distracted her and she went over. Rest in peace, Maria."

Fellow tightrope walkers, beware: keep your eyes on God.

> What good will it be for someone to gain the whole world, yet forfeit their soul? (Matt. 16:26)

6. *God hasn't shown up yet, I am lost, and He is failing me.*

Last week, I got in the car. God was calling me to get quiet and to take a walk with Him. Excited that I was doing what I felt He wanted me to, I drove far to a special place. It was closed. I circled and circled it. Lost and discouraged, I said to Him, "God, you brought me here only to get me lost."

Only then did I look down. I saw the roughly scribbled words I'd written all along the way at the many stoplights. Ones He inspired. He'd been with me all along. I wasn't lost, but in the process of being found.

If you feel lost or out of place, ask God why. There is usually more to it than meets the eye.

Point 3: Why Starting Something Doesn't Make You as Stupid as You Feel

Starting anything is hard. It almost always appears stupid and not worth tackling. But let me assure you: God doesn't think it is stupid. And He certainly doesn't despise a start. Starting is half the battle. It is the bike push that gets you gliding. It is the rope a foot above the ground.

> Do not despise these small beginnings, for the LORD rejoices to see the work begin. (Zech. 4:10 NLT)

Huge endings happen because of small beginnings. Just think, one day an Olympic gymnast first stepped on the balance beam. A missionary first opened a Bible. An author started writing a sentence that turned into a paragraph, then a story—which was probably rejected a hundred times before it got anywhere. So what? All that mattered is that one day, they decided to try to just do it. Then they kept going.

SOW A GODLY START > > >
REAP PROGRESS > > >
SEE THE GOOD GOD HAS PLANNED

The concept is simple:

If we want to reap a better body, we work out.

If we want to reap better relationships, we spend time with people.

If we want to reap a better mind, we replace tabloids with soul-building reads.

To get somewhere, we start somewhere, with a small thing, believing God, day-by-day, will take us to His somewhere.

However it looks: we put on the gym shoes that have been collecting dust in the closet. We set the alarm so time is no longer a barrier. We make the call to say "I am sorry," even when we don't want to. We write down our goals in order to step out into the dream He places in us. We mark out time in our calendar so our "action time" is permanent. We see an opening and place our toe in the door to catch hold of what God is doing.

We just do it. We take initiative.

Every good *go* has a start. So start small, and keep doing the next small thing. This leverages the law of motion. When it is still, a bike is stuck. In motion, it more easily continues to move. Objects in motion stay in motion.

Kinetic energy yields more energy. This is what we are after; it is called *momentum*. Action with momentum is sowing a life that sees results.

God encourages us to do this. He tells us to:

- Prepare our mind for action (1 Pet. 1:13).
- Put God's words into practice (and to therefore be called wise) (Matt. 7:24).
- Do much, because we've been given much (Luke 12:48).
- Live out the good works God has prepared for us (Eph. 2:10).
- Commit our works to the Lord so our plans are established (Prov. 16:3).

- Not "grow weary of doing good," for "we will reap, if we do not give up" (Gal. 6:9 ESV).

But never do it alone. Remember:

- Apart from God, we can do nothing (John 15:5).
- God gives us "the desire and the power" to please Him (Phil. 2:13 NLT).
- God gives us all we need to "abound in every good work" (2 Cor. 9:8).

ACTION + GOD'S POWER
= ABOUNDING LIFE

Our strike of trying plus God's spark starts a wildfire.

Let something new strike within you. Say to God, "I want to go all out for You." But this time, almost hear Him answering you back, saying, *So go, already.*

Then just do it. Address the call to action burning inside you, whether big or small. Whether it be a difficult marriage, off-kilter children, pride, distress, fear of the unknown, a hidden sin, a drinking habit, a dream, a ministry, a phone call, a location change, or a minor follow-through . . . no matter its size, immediately address it, with God.

Those who manage the minors become majors of the massive.

People who manage the minors don't wait around to move. Of course, they wait and seek, pray and find, but when they hear and know God is inviting them to something, they drop everything, accept His invitation, and move.

Acting immediately changes a life almost instantaneously.

I've seen it happen: hardhearted people soften, precarious situations smooth out, doors you thought were permanently closed creak open, circumstances you wrote off as impossible shed a light. Live called to action:

- If a people-group is on your heart, then learn about how you can help them.
- If you remember your neighbor with cancer, then make her soup.
- If you pray and find you can't get a friend off your mind, then reach out to her.
- If you know you need to apologize, then just do it.
- If you feel called to speak encouragement, then stop speaking criticism.
- If you've stalled on getting marriage therapy, then sign up, today.
- If you ___, then ___.

Today is your start. Starts always feel risky. Every tightrope walk of faith does. Emotions swing left and right, and you sense it won't end well. That's okay; keep walking. God is creating your path.

> You make your saving help my shield,
> and your right hand sustains me;
> your help has made me great.
> You provide a *broad path* for my feet,
> so that my ankles do not give way. (Ps. 18:35–36, emphasis added)

Keep walking. Even if at times you fall, with Christ you are never fallen.

Yes, there will be that time you snap someone's head off on Route 3. Or you scream at your kids over the mac-and-cheese dinner. Or you passive-aggressively undercut your spouse in a coffee shop. Or you gossip, even though you promised Jesus with all your heart you wouldn't. Or you forget God for a week.

Our God is a God of do-overs. He still arms you for your war with hope, a shield, the sword of the Spirit, a place of refuge, and a strong tower. Confess, accept love, and move on.

Grace is the harness on your tightrope walk called faith.

> For out of His fullness [the superabundance of His grace and truth] we have all received grace upon grace [spiritual blessing upon spiritual blessing, favor upon favor, and gift heaped upon gift]. (John 1:16 AMP)

G.R.A.C.E. is:

God
Restores
And
Catches you
Even though

Grace gives you the best of what you don't deserve because of Jesus.

Jesus—the King of Kings, Lord of Lords, Prince of Peace—died to keep you in His love. He wants you, even when you don't want yourself. He gives to you, even when you know you're unworthy. This is G.R.A.C.E.

When we joyfully receive grace—and continue on—it highlights to the world the reality of Jesus.

It is no wonder why Paul, an apostle for Jesus, told God's churches, "*Grace* and *peace* to you from God our Father and the Lord Jesus Christ" (2 Cor. 1:2, emphasis added).

These two words soften soul-crushing falls and restore God-given calls. We are wise to let them dwell within our thoughts.

1. Grace.

    Embrace it by thinking: *I am sorry, God, for_____ . Now, because of Jesus, I am seen as holy and blameless in God's sight. He accepts me and forgives my sin. It is finished and I am restored, right now, in Him, by Him, and through Him. Any residual feelings of regret, retaliation, and remorse belong to the enemy, and I choose to return those to him at this very moment.*

Grace abolishes shame.

2. Peace.

Embrace it by thinking: *Jesus left me peace and it is mine for the taking (John 14:27), so I will take it. I will receive that nothing can harm me in Christ Jesus, nothing can rule me in Christ Jesus, and nothing can stand against Christ Jesus. Indeed, Christ has set me free and I am free. This is peace.*

Peace removes fear.

To keep starting and trying, keep coming back to grace and peace.

Point 4: Ten Quick Ways to Form Long-Lasting New Habits

We've been told it takes twenty-one days to form a new habit. So we scribble January 21 on our calendar, not wanting another New Year's blowout. But it always happens. By day twenty-one, we are discouraged and doubtful; we give up. Why?

Studies prove it actually takes sixty-six days to form a new habit (with some big mess-ups along the way).[2]

Why didn't anyone ever tell me this before? I've gone nearly my whole life without this knowledge! I love this because:

1. All my failures make more sense now.
2. It takes time to really change.
3. My mess-ups don't mean I should give up. They mean I should keep going.

Beyond this, there are other ways to make positive changes stick. Let's learn them, so what God wants to form in us does.

Ten Rules for Effective Habit Change

1. **Look forward.** I believe God isn't so much concerned with you reliving your past as He is with you walking with Him in your present.

2. **Ask God for help changing.** If God is the Author and Perfecter of faith, won't He do just that? Take the pressure off your shoulders and trust His might to change you.

3. **Make God-confirmed change quickly.** Never permit your fluctuating emotions to veto your God-inspired heart.

4. **Don't overcommit.** A study has found people can sacrifice a pleasant immediate response (example: giving a rapid-fire yes in order to feel good in the moment) by considering the benefit of the future person (example: by saying no I'll be able to love my family more).[3]

   Put this into action by asking yourself: When this commitment becomes due, will I end up a love spreader or an anxiety producer? Will I love my family well? Will it tax my emotions? Will I complain because I hate that I have to do it? What are my decisions producing?

5. **Get support.** "Plans fail for lack of counsel, but with many advisers they succeed" (Prov. 15:22).

6. **Limit habit change.** Too much can feel overwhelming; just think of shopping in a store with way too many racks. Suddenly, you want to try on nothing. In the same way, if you see too much to tackle, you'll tackle nothing. Limit your habit change to one to three things at a time.

   Consider this approach with this book: hone in on a chapter, select a few points, and give it time to settle in. Too much is not good and usually results in . . . no action.

7. **Know what "flicks" you.** My daughter has a blankie. When she holds it, she likes to wet it with her mouth and rub it on her face. This then triggers her finger-sucking. Something likely triggers your bad habits:

   - A specific feeling: hunger, jealousy, inadequacy, and so forth.

   - A placement of something: a wine glass left on the counter ready for an evening pour, shoes left on the floor by a husband, and so on.

   - A person: a mean response makes you mean, and an evil eye makes you want to tell someone off.

   - A poke of an injured area of your heart: adults laugh at you the way kids used to, or someone tells you you're dumb and it reminds you of your worst fear.

   What sets you off?

8. **Re-create in your mind a new outcome.** See a new response in your mind. Speak in your mind what you might speak out loud. Address the issues that might come up beforehand.

9. **Remind yourself.** Do it with images. Do it with notes taped around the house. Do it with reminders on your phone, or with a screen saver. Do it with a bracelet that has just the right message.

   For example, if you want to spend more wisely, put a reminder where it counts: on your wallet. Draw a picture of a sad self and tape it inside, next to your cards. Remind yourself when you open that wallet how you'll feel if you waste the money you've been saving for graduate school.

10. **Get specific.** A Harvard University study shows that the more you specifically plan something (how, when, where), the more likely you will be to actually follow through on it. It reminds your mind at the right time regarding your detailed approach to accomplishing things.[4]

Bonus Tip!

Ask yourself: *What did that old habit provide for me?* (Example: watching all-night TV relaxes me.)

Now, contemplate: *How is God calling me to an equally good benefit through a completely new habit?* (Uplifting books could relax me too.)

Put it together by finding your "but instead."

> Example 1: I waste my nights watching bad reality TV because it relaxes me, "but instead" I can spend my nights reading books that bless me *and* relax me.

> Example 2: I get defensive because I feel protective, "but instead" I can feel protected by remembering God has a banner of love over me and condemnation can't stick to me. With this, I can receive and consider input while knowing I am 100 percent protected and covered in Christ.

Detail short-term and long-term goals, because what is written is kept. What is specific is seen through. What you decide decisively to do you will do.

<<< SEE >>> www.iambattleready.com to download a "Mini Battle Ready Plan" that is customizable just for you.

Point 5: Miss This and You'll Miss It All

A man once asked a tightrope walker how he accomplished the task. The tightrope walker replied, "I fix my eyes on where I'm going and never think about falling."

Fix your eyes on Jesus. Don't think about falling. Just do it.

Just DO IT

✻

YOU ARE
"*Called* TO *Action*"

✻

ACTION + GOD'S POWER =
Abounding Life

✻

Grace AND *Peace*
TO *You*

✻

FIX YOUR EYES
ON *Jesus*

A MIND TO CONQUER

Without movement, you go nowhere.

PRAY

Father, I don't want an average life. I want Your life. Will You inspire it in me? Will You teach me Your ways? Give me wisdom, understanding, and a heart to know You. Guide me in Your ways so that I can follow them. In Jesus's name. Amen.

WRITE THREE THINGS YOU'RE THANKFUL FOR

1. _____

2. _____

3. _____

ENTER YOUR MIND

Do you ever say, "If I can't make a big splash, I don't want to do it"?

It turns out more wins are better than huge wins. The author and director of the Persuasive Tech Lab at Stanford University notes that if we pick small and quantifiable wins, we can more easily win and create an internal celebration when we do.[5]

What would it look like for you to win in a small way? What would it look like for you to commemorate your small or big wins? How could you celebrate and make something of them? Write it down. How can you be faithful to what you commit to?

EXAMINE YOUR STORY

1. What fear holds you back from moving forward?
2. How have you let the world, critiques, or opinions hold you back?

112

3. How do your high expectations of yourself actually restrict you?

4. How have you subconsciously told yourself God is at fault?

5. What would it look like to make life change? What habit-forming tips could you implement to see things through?

EXPLORE WITH GROUP STUDY

1. What did you learn from your personal study time?

2. What have you restrained yourself from doing? Why? What do you dream of doing?

3. Where do you fall on the spectrum: dead faith or wild, almost scandalous faith?

4. Read Isaiah 61:1–7. What if this was your year of favor? If you really believed God was going to do this in your life, how would you approach things differently? How would you go all-in?

5. Pick one new thing to start doing. Share it within the group. Be accountable to each other next week. Check in on that item. Set a reminder to check in again in a couple weeks.

6. Discuss the various ways Jesus chose to act when he could have chosen to please man, stay in good standing with the government, preserve Himself, make His disciples think highly of Him, or come off as a king.

   How did Jesus see things through? What did He pursue? What mattered most?

   How can you be like Jesus?

7. What is the difference between hard-driving activity and God-inspired activity? How can you recognize the difference in your life?

8. Share together what grace is. Share specific examples of it.

   (Example: Grace is God telling me He'll help me next time when I yell at the kids. Grace is the idea I am in God's favor even when I feel down on myself.)

113

9. Pray for each other one by one. Ask God to help you go, do, love, and serve as Jesus did.

10. Talk about your specific action plan to break or change a habit. How will you leverage the habit-changing tips to do so?

A CHRIST-CENTERED PRINCIPLE
GOD BLESSES

Activity founded in love

Greater love has no one than this: to lay down one's life for one's friends. (John 15:13)

⤜⤜⤜ ---- Warrior Mind-Set Five ---- ⟶

*It's Not about How Low You Go for God
as Much as It Is How Near to
His Embrace You Stay*

(Humility)

The world clamors, "Do more! Be all that you can be!" But
our Father whispers, "Be still and know that I am God."

Joanna Weaver,
Having a Mary Heart in a Martha World

Point 1: A Modern-Day Woman's Epidemic: Slapping the Hand of God

Imagine this: you are invited to the dinner party of all dinner
parties. Upon your arrival, the Host opens the door. You inhale.
You smell the courses to come. The scent of herbs, warmth, and
love are pouring out of the unseen kitchen. It is almost edible.
You hunger for it. The Host invites you in, so you follow His lead.

He whispers to you, "I hope you like what you see; I have prepared all of this for you, in advance. I have gone to great lengths
to secure this—for you, dear." He smiles.

Is that excitement you see in His eyes? They look pure. Upon arrival to the dining patio, He gestures to your seat. There, you see it. How did He know? Your favorite color, royal blue, adorns the table. Hues of gold seem to highlight everything your heart loves. He has richly given. Hydrangeas overflow onto the table. They mesmerize you.

"Beautiful daughter, this is all for you."

It's brilliant, you silently agree. Far more brilliant than you ever knew was possible. He even knew to decorate with twinkle lights overhead. You love twinkle lights.

And the music. Oh, the music! It is an instrumental orchestra of something amazing. Everything is alive at this "dream dinner." Your thoughts are distracted as you notice your plate. There is an envelope on it with your name. You know He's written valuable things about your life. You want to see, to rip it open and discover all He has to say.

But you get caught up in what happens next. In comes the platters of the freshest seafood, the most delectable delights, and lush vegetables. It is all you want. You hunger.

Your eyes focus on Him, and you want to experience the fullness of everything He is, everything He has done and is doing. You desire to clench on to Him and to know all about it.

That is, until you catch a glimpse of yourself. Your normal and ordinary self. Then your shoulders slump; your fear mounts. *What's His interest in all this? What does He want from me? What am I going to have to do or give up to get all this?* You look at your feet.

You consider how small and weak you are. You remember how others have treated you. You decide, *He couldn't possibly want to be with me, without strings attached.*

This wasn't all meant for me. It couldn't be. Forget Him.

You drop His hand. And run.

You try not to look back, but you do. And as you do, you catch His eyes. They beckon you back. You see the scars in His hands.

They remind you of the cost of all this. But you can't go back. You can't turn around now.

Instead you think, *I don't deserve this. I am not good enough. This couldn't have been meant for me. Doesn't He know who I am? Plus, I didn't even bring a gift. I'd be a taker and not a giver.*

Pride makes you run, even though you know all you ever needed, wanted, or hoped is there with Him, with Jesus.

You slapped God's loving hand away. You missed God's incredibility because of a side-glance at all your inadequacies. Worst of all, in some ways, you did it under the Pharisaical guise of humility.

Beware: insecurity does not equal humility.

Point 2: The True Reason You Always Feel Left Out

I've heard people say God is a gentleman. It is true. Jesus doesn't force His way on us. He opens the door and invites us somewhere. Whether we walk through or not usually depends on if we focus on His sacrifice, His wounds, His price . . . if we remember the price of love.

Today, what is God inviting you into?

Sometimes, we as women get messages like:

Come with presents in hand, then you can accept good things.

Come as you are, but don't show off.

Give, but never take too much or you'll be selfish.

Enjoy the moment, but don't take it too far or you'll steal God's glory.

Dance, but don't steal the show—pride goes before the fall!

Speak, but not too loud or you won't look ladylike.

As a result, it feels like we must constantly appease *those types* who keep track of the wrongs we may make at any moment. Doing this is a full-time job in and of itself, one Jesus didn't call us to.

God says:

"Let your light shine before others, that they may see your good
deeds and glorify your Father in heaven" (Matt. 5:16).

"You are the light of the world. A town built on a hill cannot
be hidden" (v. 14).

"Neither do people light a lamp and put it under a bowl. Instead
they put it on its stand, and it gives light to everyone in the
house" (v. 15).

God never told us to climb into our self, in fear; He told us to
climb out into the world—with world-changing, radical, monstrous
love. Yet often our shame goes before us, rather than Jesus's love.
We don't want to get prideful, so we do nothing. We don't want
to accidentally sin, so we stay where we are. We stay stuck. Like
a wounded bird.

I believe this is sin.

Do we fault our kid for getting an A? Do we mock one who has
stepped out into foreign lands to save millions? Why do we stomp
on our God-given dreams?

Why do we limit ourselves and others? Who are we to judge,
to pull down, to hold back, to limit, to question, to fix, to de-
termine, to opine, or to decide? Since when did we become the
enemy-accuser?

We speak things like . . .

She's doing amazing paintings . . . humph! Show-off!

Sure, she's serving the poor, but she sure doesn't look like she's
serving her husband that much.

She may be excelling in mothering, but her car looks like it
hasn't been washed in weeks.

She may be going to graduate school, but I hope she fails.

She may be confident in her skin—but, oh, at least I am not
prideful like her.

Or . . .

That's never been done before.

Don't do that. That is not a good idea.

I don't think God wants you to do that.

Well, I think . . .

Who are you to think you can do that? It's too lofty, too godly, too . . .

When we speak limiting things to others, we actually limit our self. Our thoughts set into the mind-mold we've created through our words. Then when it is our turn to step out, those exact thoughts fall right out onto our own lap. Our attempt at action is thwarted.

REAP NEGATIVE WORDS TOWARD OTHERS > > > SOW INTERNAL SELF-DOUBT > > > SEE YOUR LIFE STUCK

This road-blocking of ourselves and others pains me. If we only see skin, how can we judge what God is doing within someone's heart? Who are we to judge when God just might be up to His best work ever?

As a sisterhood, can we agree to stop being our own worst enemy? Can we relinquish the role of sizing up and feeling sized up?

Jesus, I believe, doesn't want us held back.

Jesus, I believe, knows our time is limited. That we need each other to live out these grand and glorious callings. That we are not in charge of others' humility. And that humility is often found by trial and error.

But if humility never tries, it's always in error. It submits to pride, in fear.

It slaps away nail-scarred hands.

It misses His invitations, His lessons, His refinement, His grace, His relationship, His heart, His ways, His plan, His portion, His peace.

Jesus's table is set. But we can't easily accept God's good when we're only thinking of how *she* needs to improve.

I know this type of hand-slapping pride far too well. "Want prayer?" a friend recently said to me. Embarrassed by my struggle, and not wanting to be seen as weak, I wanted to feign happiness and turn away. I didn't. Thank God! *The Gentleman was extending me an invitation through my friend.*

Another time, in the kitchen, pots and pans filled the sink while others were burning on the stove. The kids were starving. I was too. Tensions were rising. All I wanted was a moment to sit, to rest. My husband turned toward me and said, "Kelly, can I help you?" This time? Because I wanted the extra emotional benefits that come with being a victim, I snapped back, "No! I've got it." *The Gentleman was extending me an invitation through my husband.*

Not too long ago, an opportunity came my way, yet to fully embrace it I needed to share on social media. I also needed to let myself out of the box and do a video to support it. I knew, with my all-out, fully seen efforts behind it, it would take flight. But I was scared to shine. I was afraid of what others might think. *The Gentleman was extending me an invitation through social media.*

What invitations have you turned away?

Imagine, for a moment, if Matthew, Mark, Luke, or John shut down their super-effective ministry shop because they

feared others would think they were show-offs for Jesus,

worried they were too seen in Scripture and, therefore, were
stealing glory from God,

were embarrassed and ashamed before a God who saw they
weren't model citizens, or

were fraught with anxiety over the idea they were not as good
as Jesus.

We've named fear *humility* and turned away from God's best.
No longer. Our aim is not to be understood by other people but
to be in service to Jesus Christ, no matter the cost.

Point 3: The Either-Or Decisions That'll Bless or Distress You

So what should we do at this point? Move out and steamroll everything and everyone in our way? No.

We take the low seat.

The one Jesus invites us to.

> But when you are invited, take the lowest place, so that when your
> host comes, he will say to you, "Friend, move up to a better place."
> Then you will be honored in the presence of all the other guests.
> (Luke 14:10)

To take the low seat looks like pulling away from your busy
day to meet Jesus. It looks like getting into the confines of your
bedroom to pray over what He's calling you to do. It looks like
confessing your sins and searching your heart. It looks like hearing His Word come alive in a way that changes you. It looks like
dropping everything to stand up and shine in life, if that is what
He wants.

It looks like being Peter at the Last Supper. Like getting your
feet washed by love.

> So [Jesus] got up from the meal, took off his outer clothing, and
> wrapped a towel around his waist. After that, he poured water into

a basin and began to wash his disciples' feet, drying them with the towel that was wrapped around him.

He came to Simon Peter, who said to him, "Lord, are you going to wash my feet?"

Jesus replied, "You do not realize now what I am doing, but later you will understand."

"No," said Peter, "you shall never wash my feet."

Jesus answered, "Unless I wash you, you have no part with me." (John 13:4–8)

Never miss in pride what God has for you to learn through humility. Surely Peter could have said, "I am not worthy. I cannot allow myself to sit next to the King of Kings; I cannot accept that He makes me worthy. I mess up too much. I will look like a show-off to those not invited. Jesus is leagues better than me, and He'll make me feel bad about myself. I'll never match up to Him, so why bother? Thanks but no thanks. I am afraid I'll steal the show, the glory, from you, God."

But Peter accepted. He took a low seat, so humility could teach him.

Do we? Or do we say, "I'll not be like her, or them. All those show-offs. I'll deny people's words of encouragement, of confidence building. I'll remember how I really might sin at any moment if I try to do something good, or how I'll fail. While everyone else shows off, I won't. I'll be better than that. I will stay far from that. I'll lie down, even. I'll decline His offer, then lie down."

And go nowhere. Miss His feast. Miss the washing, the cleansing of dirty shame, and the falling off of self as Jesus purifies us through His miraculous hands.

We *cannot* miss—any longer—what God has set up for us.

So let us not be deceived. Not like I am . . . when I'm afraid to be me at Bible study because I don't want to appear to be too much or not enough. Or when I get intimidated by a woman who seems to be so great she highlights I am nothing. Or when I call it honoring God but underneath am desperately nervous about how I "come off." Or when I try to lie about the exciting things happening because I don't want you to feel threatened.

I believe these slap God's hand and kill invitations.

What are your invitation killers? Dream-crushing fears? Do you overthink? Procrastinate? What might it look like to let Love attend to you?

> When he had finished washing their feet, he put on his clothes and returned to his place. "Do you understand what I have done for you?" he asked them. "You call me 'Teacher' and 'Lord,' and rightly so, for that is what I am. Now that I, your Lord and Teacher, have washed your feet, you also should wash one another's feet. I have set you an example *that you should do as I have done for you*." (John 13:12–15, emphasis added)

True humility accepts then blesses humanity. Insecurity sits in the basement, all proud it isn't sinning or making a fool of itself.

One releases love. The other is entrapped within its own error.

Point 4: Three Ways to Align Your Mind with Christ's

"We love because he first loved us" (1 John 4:19). Don't get confused. We don't work hard via our own manpower and become credentialed to receive His love.

I love my son no more today than yesterday, even if today he cleaned the whole house.

Work can't work up more love. Indeed, God loves obedience. But think for a moment: Who of us loves the feeling of being loved because of someone else's burdening guilt, pestering shame, or obligation? That kind of love is different.

"If I give all I possess to the poor and give over my body to hardship that I may boast, but do not have love, I gain nothing" (1 Cor. 13:3).

God is love. Love sourced from God is love. We hug because He hugged us. We sympathize because He sympathized with us. We encourage others because His encouragement has filled us.

Jesus on us rubs off on others.

How is Jesus in you rubbing off on others?

There is no pressure here. I imagine some of you are thinking of what to improve on and how to work things out for God. What host demands his houseguests do the dishes after eating? Or sends them home because their housewarming gift didn't equate to the meal?

Jesus is not one who demands worth; He is the man who gives worth, unduly.

Do you conjure up works or connect to His love? Let Him address your needs or only address others'?

Sometimes we think we are doing things right, but in humility we learn we are not.

Jesus, dying in humility, spoke, "Father, forgive [your name here], for she knows not what she does" (see Luke 23:34).

Forgive her; I love her. Forgive her; I will take her place. Forgive her; I want her. Forgive her; may she accept what I have done. Forgive her; may she believe what I say about her.

Amazingly, Jesus rose up strong so we could lay down low, in complete need of His love. Dependent, we take His life and eat of it—peace, hope, joy, love. We become filled with His sacrifice and ready to sacrifice. We see what we usually cannot see. We uncover the wild moves of God we've always hoped for.

True connection with Jesus is uniting to His humility, His love, His life, His covering, and His ways, until we're sure all we want is Him. Until our dim candle begins to rage like a wildfire.

Then, we more readily say:

Jesus, forgive me.

Jesus, love me.

Jesus, teach me Your heart.

Practical Application Ideas

- Take an inventory of your emotions through the day. Talk with Jesus about them. When something is off-putting, bring it to Jesus.

- Recognize when you feel weak. In that moment, ask God to give you insight and wisdom on how He makes you strong.

- Consider God's closeness. He is not far. The Holy Spirit lives in you and desires to lead you.

Jesus, I want less of me.

Jesus, I'll leave it all behind.

Jesus, You are my best gift.

Jesus. Jesus. Jesus. I welcome You. I want You. Change me. Teach me. Everything else tastes bland in comparison to You.

We accept the invitation, like John did at Jesus's last supper. Scripture says, "One of His disciples, whom Jesus loved (esteemed), was leaning against Jesus' chest (John 13:23 AMP).

Disciples loved by Jesus lean against Him.

I want to live my life leaning on Jesus.

John didn't turn away in fear, thinking others would call him a show-off, selfish, or arrogant. He wasn't debilitated by his own weakness. He took the extravagant opportunity to love and be loved. He rested on Him who is Rest. Without shame and without overwhelming regrets.

Humility lets someone love you.

To get you going, let's consider three ways to welcome God's love.

1. Desperately need Him. I notice when I'm physically hungry but rarely notice when I'm spiritually hungry. You too? We

125

can easily feed our bodies while paying no attention to our inner temples. We notice we're tired yet forget to ask God for help. We do our daily routine while never asking if this is what God wants from us. What if we desperately desired God as much as we desired to have a good day?

2. Listen for Him. Meeting points for God are all around: God's Word, a chance to rediscover your childlike nature as you dance with your kids, a fresh coffee alone on the porch on a fog-dense morning, a prayer walk that can change the path

Pulling Closer

- Remember what you loved to do as a girl, then do it with God. Awaken a curious, experiential nature in you that wants to soak in what God is teaching. Do art, song, dance—whatever you once loved.

- Choose to see the very best of God in others. Be a Pollyanna of sorts. Rather than seeing others' worst, choose to see God's best. See, even if it's very faint, what Jesus would see. Who knows? You may even make a new friend.

- Let go of personal attacks. You can't hear the voice of love when your mind is full of wrathful thoughts about another.

- Try not to shy away from your mistakes. Rather, in humility, embrace them to see what you can learn.

- Stop constantly apologizing for everything you do. Example: Instead of saying, "I am sorry I made you late," say, "Thank you for bearing with me as I took a little extra time." Exchange *sorry* for *thank you*. Some of us live constantly sorry; it is hard to rejoice and be thankful in this stance.

of your life, a drive to the location where you first fell in love with your husband. Our God is a God who still leads, prompts, and directs today. Understand where your connection point is and be open to the fact that sometimes it may feel like a moving target. That's okay; adjust.

3. Recount His goodness. Recount a time God made the impossible possible. Relive it. Feel it. Emotionalize it to help your brain become reacquainted with it. Remember the details. What comes to mind? What did it teach you about God? How might it help you in the future?

Point 5: Why Love Ricochets and Always Hits You Back

Love is not contained. It is uncontainable. As the world sees the face of love, it can't help but change its face.

UNLEASH DAM > > > FLOW
(REAP > > > SEE)

This is what we want. We want Christ in us to flow out from us.

Whoever believes in me, as Scripture has said, rivers of living water will flow from within them. (John 7:38)

We want to be fountains. Because when Christ's love flows in, it flows out.

Consider the blind man in John 9 whom Jesus healed. Jesus's great love compelled the man to run into the streets, virtually proclaiming, "I can see! I can see!" Consider Peter, the mess-up who denied Jesus three times. He preached with extreme anointing and

Pulling Closer

- Write down every time God has been faithful.
- Thank God for every time He has been faithful.
- Notice the themes of your life and how He has been faithful.
- Praise Him for how He will once again be faithful to you today and tomorrow.
- Recognize how He is faithful in the Bible.

saving power after being restored by the love of Jesus. Consider the woman at the well who left her water jar and went into the city to say, "Come, see a man who told me everything I ever did. Could this be the Messiah?" (John 4:28–29). Or the man with a demon who "went away and told all over town how much Jesus had done for him" (Luke 8:39).

Christ's love speaks up and draws attention. Then a world of hate listens. People wonder, "How?"

Love Apparent is what moves people. Isn't it what moved you to accept Jesus as your Lord? A taste of love compels our heart to leave it all for another helping: "Again, the kingdom of heaven is like a merchant looking for fine pearls. When he found one of great value, he went away and sold everything he had and bought it" (Matt. 13:45–46).

What is love calling you to leave behind? Very likely it is not your house, car, or clothes, but it is certainly something meaningful. Perhaps an attitude? A posture? A habit? A thing you can't stop clinging to? Something you can't give up?

When Jesus had called the Twelve together, he gave them power and authority to drive out all demons and to cure diseases, and he sent them out to proclaim the kingdom of God and to heal the sick. He told them: "Take nothing for the journey—no staff, no bag, no bread, no money, no extra shirt." (Luke 9:1–3)

You need nothing when you have everything: Jesus. His love can make room for our new reality. Love.

UNLEASH DAM > > > FLOW
GET INVITATION > > > RIP IT OPEN > > >
JUST DO IT > > > LOVE

How? Get near Him. Move with Him. Be full of His Word. Let His fruit be your high desire. Let His life become your metric. Let His goals be your vision. Let His sacrifice make way for yours. Let His memories become your memories. Let His hope consume you. Let His heart refine you. Let His humility teach you. Don't be afraid to let Him flood your world.

Let the Living Water spread, which water does by nature. Test it: pour some on your kitchen counter.

Love spreads. It also returns back to us. Take note of how this happens in the world:

1. Love sparks chain reactions. Some time ago, a man gave up his kidney, and then so did many others all around the country. Love almost can't help but multiply.

2. Givers get a giver high. When we help in kindness, dopamine fires off and we feel great!

3. Being generous keeps us young. As we are kind, loving, and giving, oxytocin increases while free radicals decrease, and we fend off aging.

4. Our hearts grow stronger. Jealousy injures our heart with stress and increased blood pressure. Yet loving others protects our heart as it releases oxytocin. It also builds more love within us as our relationships improve.[1]

5. Love boomerangs. As we are authentic and vulnerable with others, they actually love us more for it. People love people with flaws.

What might God be calling you to give? Your time? Your heart? Your education? Your money? Your encouragement?

Friends, we can't ever out-give God. "Give, and it will be given to you. A good measure, pressed down, shaken together and running over, will be poured into your lap. For with the measure you use, it will be measured to you" (Luke 6:38). What love we throw out boomerangs back at us.

But, to send out love, we must first sow it in our mind. Here are four ways to seize a L.O.V.E. mentality:

1. **Let go of can'ts, won'ts, and shouldn'ts.**

   Instead of thinking: I can't possibly deserve this. I won't; there are so many who are better than me. I shouldn't; I will appear arrogant if I do this. . . .

   Start affirming: God wants me to always rejoice. He wants me to rejoice in the good things He has set before me—the opportunities, the missions, and the blessings—as much as the difficult things—the trials, the tears, and the deaths. Today, I choose to say You are a great God with great plans, and I will trust You, even when it is awkward. I accept Your invitation.

   Rejoice in the Lord always. I will say it again: Rejoice! (Phil. 4:4)

2. **Open the flow.**

Instead of thinking: I must get ahead of the day. I don't have time to sit with Jesus. I am all alone. I must do things for God in order to be loved. I must appear like I have it all together.

Start spending time with God, then affirming: I am one with Christ. He loves me and His love will never fail me. I am full of His Word and will choose to remember it. Thank You, God; You keep me in You.

I am the vine; you are the branches. If you remain in me and I in you, you will bear much fruit; apart from me you can do nothing. (John 15:5)

3. **Veer back to God.**

Instead of thinking: I should be doing what she is doing. I am not as good as him. She is a step ahead. I need to get his opinion. She needs to tell me what to do. I will never find my way. Society proves this is the way to go.

Start praying: God, bless her. God, help him. God, I see these good qualities in her. Bless her with every good thing. I trust You, and aside from You, God, I have no want. You have the best way for me. I believe. I am Yours. Your will leads me to my deepest desires. On this I stand. You will never lead me wrong.

I will instruct you and teach you in the way you should go; I will counsel you with my loving eye on you. (Ps. 32:8)

4. **Expect God to show up and to show up *big*!**

Instead of thinking: My life will always look like this. Things will always stay as they are. I'll never change. God is far away. The days are all the same.

Start affirming, internally and externally: My God is a powerful God. He is a mighty God. He is an ever-moving God. As I do His will, I will see His incredible love. As I follow Him, He will do things I never expected. God will answer my prayer. I will see the goodness of the Lord.

He is "able to do immeasurably more than all we ask or imagine, according to his power that is at work within us" (Eph. 3:20). Choose to be an invitation-accepting giver. Don't do it solely because you know love boomerangs but do it because His love can't help but flow out of you.

A generous person will prosper; whoever refreshes others will be refreshed. (Prov. 11:25)

Now he who supplies seed to the sower and bread for food will also supply and increase your store of seed and will enlarge the harvest of your righteousness. (2 Cor. 9:10)

And God is able to bless you abundantly, so that in all things at all times, having all that you need, you will abound in every good work. (2 Cor. 9:8)

The LORD bestows favor and honor; no good thing does he withhold from those whose walk is blameless. (Ps. 84:11)

<<< ACCEPT >>> God's best invitations. Discover "12 Ways to Intimately Experience God" at www.iambattleready.com.

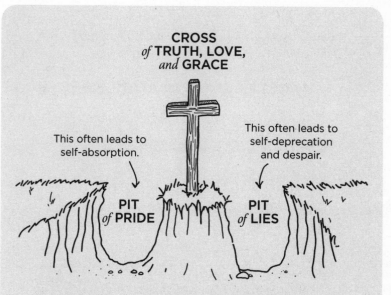

CROSS
of **TRUTH, LOVE,**
and **GRACE**

This often leads to
self-absorption.

This often leads to
self-deprecation
and despair.

PIT
of **PRIDE**

PIT
of **LIES**

We are usually more okay living in the pit of lies
than the pit of pride, but where we should rest
is under the truth of Jesus Christ.

What to Remember:

INSECURITY DOES NOT EQUAL HUMILITY

ACCEPT GOD'S INVITATIONS

HUMILITY LEANS ON JESUS

UNLEASH DAM >>> FLOW

YOU CAN'T EVER OUT-GIVE GOD

LOVE LASTS

HAVE A L.O.V.E. MIND-SET

Jesus Principle

To abide in Christ, you have to find alone time with Him. May I remind you? Even Jesus rested. He spent time alone (Luke 5:16). He got away to pray (Mark 6:46). He renewed Himself with Scripture (Matt. 4:1–11). He laid back and took a break (Mark 4:35–40).

Go low and trust your Provider to provide.

A MIND TO CONQUER

If you know God's interest is you,
you'll give full interest to what His mind calls you to do.

PRAY

Lord, I want to be close to You and live with You so I can speak like You, hear like You, love like You, and talk like You. I can't do it alone. I need You more than life itself. Come to me with power, strength, and fresh resolve. Fill me, Holy Spirit, with Your power so I have the power to do the will of God in this world. In Jesus's name. Amen.

WRITE THREE THINGS YOU'RE THANKFUL FOR

1. _____

2. _____

3. _____

ENTER YOUR MIND

Ellen Hendriksen notes there are three toxic patterns of thinking that really do us in.[2] In humility, ask yourself, *Do I do these things?*

1. Live with emotional reasoning: "This toxic thinking habit mistakes feelings for reality. If you feel guilty, it must be your fault. If you feel hopeless, there must be no way out. If you feel anxious, something bad is about to happen."

2. Resort to mind-reading others: "Mind reading makes you think others are either judging or rejecting you. 'He didn't text me back so he must hate me.' 'My boss wants to see me so she must be mad.' 'Everyone will see I'm sweating and think I'm a freak.'"

3. Constantly personalize issues: "The thinking error of personalization makes everything about you. Your spouse is grumpy, so you assume it's something you did."

EXAMINE YOUR STORY

1. In what ways do you slap away the hand of God? Think of a time when you have done this.

2. When do you specifically feel unworthy to accept from God? From others? Think of your own stories.

3. In what ways do you hold yourself back so people don't think you are too much, too [fill in the blank], or simply not enough?

EXPLORE WITH GROUP STUDY

1. What did you learn from your personal study time?

2. How do these words compel you to step out? If you fully believed God was your shield and strength, and that nothing could touch you, what would you do?

Praise be to the LORD,
> for he has heard my cry for mercy.
The LORD is my strength and my shield;
> my heart trusts in him, and he helps me.
My heart leaps for joy,
> and with my song I praise him.
The LORD is the strength of his people,
> a fortress of salvation for his anointed one.
Save your people and bless your inheritance;
> be their shepherd and carry them forever. (Ps. 28:6–9)

3. What does the cross mean to you? To being humble? To stepping out?
4. In what ways can you foster
   - a needy heart?
   - a listening and receptive heart?
   - a goodness-centered heart?
5. What are some of the drawbacks of false pride?
6. What are some of the benefits of true humility?
7. In order to L.O.V.E., what do you sense God calling you to do differently?
8. How can you be like the apostle John? What would this look like practically?
9. How might doing this change your life?

A CHRIST-CENTERED PRINCIPLE GOD BLESSES

Humility that trusts God no matter what

Blessed are the poor in spirit, for theirs is the kingdom of heaven. . . .
Blessed are the meek, for they will inherit the earth. (Matt. 5:3, 5)

It's Not What Your Eyes See,
but What the Eyes of Your Heart See,
That Lets You See Everything

(Objectivity)

We see the world, not as it is, but as we are—or, as we are conditioned to see it.

Stephen R. Covey,
The 7 Habits of Highly Effective People

Point 1: Six Self-Reflection Questions That Bring Clarity

The phone rang.

The lady I called answered, saying, "Hello," but before I could answer back she said, "I am not interested. Take me off your list."

Click.

Baffled, I stayed on the line and continued talking. "Wait, uhh . . . I am just trying to call for a recommendation on a babysitter . . ."

Dead air. She was long gone.

Long gone. She translated my call wrong, thinking I was a telemarketer. I wasn't. But this lady knew *her own truth*. Because of this, she acted on it.

Standing there with a dead phone in my hands, I was struck by how she got things so wrong.

Later, after I texted her, we talked. Essentially she said, "My past made me afraid. When you called, I figured you were a telemarketer."

Her faulty translation dictated her actions. Equally, our faulty translations cause bad actions when we forgo truth and settle on reacting to a half-truth (lie). This is how we hurt others and get hurt ourselves.

How often do you react with an impulsive translation?
Take inventory.

1. When aggravation mounts with others, do you actively look for what is good (their intentions, God in them, their redeeming qualities)? Or do you just see what frustrates you and unleash your temper?

   > You realize, don't you, that you are the temple of God, and God himself is present in you? No one will get by with vandalizing God's temple, you can be sure of that. God's temple is sacred—and you, remember, *are* the temple. (1 Cor. 3:16–17 MSG)

2. Are you mentally engaged in your day as an offensive player on God's team, or do you sit on the sidelines as a defensive victim?

   > For we are both God's workers. And you are God's field. (1 Cor. 3:9 NLT)

   If we're put in the game, we don't go back to sit on the sidelines. We know what we were sent out to do, so we run into the pack, the sweaty mess, and we do our best.

3. Do you pursue issues of your heart? Or do you constantly wonder, *What's wrong with them?*

> Therefore judge nothing before the appointed time; wait
> until the Lord comes. He will bring to light what is hid-
> den in darkness and will expose the motives of the heart.
> (1 Cor. 4:5)

4. Do you constantly count up the world's bad actions? Or do
   you look for ways that you can take action to bring peace?
   Paul contended with this:

> Even now we go hungry and thirsty, and we don't have
> enough clothes to keep warm. We are often beaten and
> have no home. We work wearily with our own hands
> to earn our living. We bless those who curse us. We are
> patient with those who abuse us. We appeal gently when
> evil things are said about us. Yet we are treated like the
> world's garbage, like everybody's trash—right up to the
> present moment. (1 Cor. 4:11–13 NLT)

But he still kept a mentality that focused on this: "I press
on toward the goal to win the prize for which God has called
me heavenward in Christ Jesus" (Phil. 3:14).

And his life resulted in this: many were saved, many lands
were reached, and even today the story of Jesus continues
to spread.

5. Are you known by your Facebook critiques? Or by your love?

> By this everyone will know that you are my disciples, if
> you love one another. (John 13:35)

6. Is your life shaped by what you see before you? Or by the
   God above you? His promises? His view? His attitudes? His
   perceptions? His callings? His plans?

> Whoever has ears, let them hear what the Spirit says to
> the churches. (Rev. 2:29)

Love wants to speak to your families, to your friends, and to your very own heart.

7. Do you immediately get offended by others and walk away from them? Or do you spend time trying to understand their perspective in order to work through the problem?

Love is patient, love is kind. (1 Cor. 13:4)

There is almost always more than meets the eye. Jesus often said, "Whoever has ears, let them hear" (Matt. 11:15). He also noted that people "look, but they don't really see. They hear, but they don't really listen or understand" (Matt. 13:13 NLT).

Let us not be deaf and blind. A partial truth is still a partial lie.

Point 2: Why Bad Eyesight Perpetuates Horrible Feelings

Life easily gets lost in translation. If the GPS directions say "turn left" but you translate the voice to say "turn right," you'll go the wrong way. And get lost.

There's no quicker way to go where you don't want to go than to translate things wrong. It happens all the time. We misread a person's countenance. We misunderstand what was said. We assume the worst.

Mazda once named a car "Laputa," but they didn't understand translation. Apparently, that word meant "the whore" in Spanish. I am sure they never set off to be offensive; their translation was faulty.

Bad translations equal big problems.

Especially when what *isn't* happening, we presume or assume is. Or what *is* happening, we think isn't (denial and rationalization). Here, we tend to act on lies.

Our mind can easily deceive us. Ever been in a car and thought you were moving backward, only to find out it was the car next to you moving forward? Ever gotten off a boat and still felt your body rocking? Ever hurt a body part and still acted like it was injured long after it was healed?

Beneath the Surface

There is always more than meets the eye. Yet often we fail to realize this. Instead we notice . . .

A "look" from another woman. *She is angry at me because I didn't sympathize enough with her problems.*

The lack of texts from a friend. *She doesn't really think I add that much to our relationship.*

The expressions on our kids' faces at dinnertime. *They hate all my food and think I am a horrible mother.*

The welcoming interest of another woman. *She already has a million friends, I am sure, and would never really want to hang out with me.*

The ordinary comment of our husband. *He thinks I am not doing a good job.*

The random remark of a family member. *She is trying to send me a backhanded message.*

But what if we've translated these things wrong? Maybe the "look" is because she is thinking about her own difficult life at home. The lack of texts is because all of us are busy. The faces at dinnertime are because the kids are tired. The interest from that woman is because she really likes you. The ordinary comment is just an ordinary comment, and the random remark was never directed at you.

Perceptions, assumptions, and judgments prevent us from seeing the heart of the story. But the heart is always what God cares for most.

So we write a person off, labeling her offensive; meanwhile there is a whole lengthy, tear-soaked backstory that had nothing to do

Test Your Translation

What is this?   **Pronounce this.**

Say the name of it out loud.   Say the name of it out loud.

Did you say pee-can?   How did you say it?
Or pe-can?   May-uh-naze or man-aze?

Translations impact what comes out of our mouth.

with us and everything to do with the deep pain in her. We miss the depth of relationship God was prepared to bring. We miss a ministry opportunity, many times.

In nearly every case, faulty translations see one angle, *our own*. But there are other angles to see from:

1. When you look in the mirror, you notice the deep wrinkles, the age spots, and the droopy eyes. You depressively tell yourself you're expendable.

    New angle: You laugh a lot. You smile a lot. You've lived life with all your heart. You have wisdom to share with the world. You wear life well.

2. You work as a waitress to put yourself through school. Yet all you can think, as everyone else is getting their master's degrees and PhDs is: *I'm dumb*. And you're missing out on life because you're not doing more.

    New angle: You are investing in your future. To get somewhere requires sacrifices. There is a purpose to where you are today, and God has plans to use you right where you are.

3. People hurt your feelings again. People always let you down.

    New angle: People are people. They are not perfect. God is. *I can choose to let God's Word define me in such great magnitude that other people's actions and reactions don't injure me so.*

There is more than meets the eye. It is all about our perception.

A Buffet Lifestyle

This reminds me of my son. He used to always protect his food. He would grip the last piece of cookie, saving it, not letting anyone touch it. Until the day I took him to a buffet. It gave him a new translation. From a new angle, he looked over at me, across the table, and perceived, "Mommy, I have so much, any treat I have on my plate is yours. Try some!" His perception changed. Rather than pulling his plate toward himself and not sharing, he knew the abundance of the buffet would take care of him if he became hungry again.

Likewise, even if we've been wronged, misunderstood, treated poorly, or maligned, we can trust the abundance of God's goodness to take care of us. In this, we can minister to others in a vulnerable, heart-forward way.

You see, God has set a buffet of goodness before us, not lack. Like my son, we can seize a "buffet mind-set," which helps us to realize:

- We can trust God to change people. We don't have to badger them.
- God takes good, good care of us. We don't need answers to our every question.
- God is for us, behind us, and with us. We don't have to cover our tracks or justify our bad actions.
- God has our answer. We don't have to run away from hard relationships.
- God is uniquely working and transforming our mind. Others don't always have to agree with us.
- Christ's power is perfected in our weakness. We don't have to distance our heart from God because of our emotions.
- Because God gives us every good thing, we are already equipped with good translations. We just need to choose to leverage them.

Need more?

- God trains our fingers for battle.
- God's love never fails.
- We are being renewed daily.

146

- We can come confidently before Christ with our every single request.
- God will renew our strength.
- The Holy Spirit will counsel us.
- We can do all things through Christ who gives us strength.

Buffet mind-sets have a million angles from which they can see the working-goodness of God.

Point 3: How to Start Seeing from Jesus's Angle

Many of us see what we:

1. Have always seen.
2. Expect to see.
3. Want to see (because it keeps things easy).

For example, some of us hate broccoli because we always have. We have no friends because we think we're a stinky friend. Truth is, we haven't given broccoli a chance ever, nor friendship in ten years.

Many times we don't see change because we don't really want to.

What do you expect to see? What one-way story is alive in your mind?

We don't want to live like the journalists of this age. We want to avoid writing one-way, slanted stories of our own. Why? Because our loud opinions tend to speak over God's quietly unfolding story. Plus, we only see an inch of the angle God does. We see a person's actions; God sees that person's thousand yesterdays, what He's got up His sleeve for their tomorrow, how meanly their brother treated them, and the mighty restoration He has coming for them five days from now. He's working in them. Or maybe He is doing work in you.

Either way, just because we cannot immediately see what God is working doesn't mean He isn't.

Remember: let's not be deaf and blind.

We want to see from Jesus's angle by considering people's histories, looking into the heart of the matter, and giving space for new understanding.

Beyond this, Jesus's life and time of testing teaches us specific ways to see from His angle during even the hardest of times. Let's take a look. . . .

- Satan *held out stones* before Jesus. Jesus was physically hungry. Satan tempted him with bread (Matt. 4:3). While I am sure Jesus's flesh wanted to change those stones to bread, He didn't.

  The Way, the Truth, and the Life angle: Jesus spoke God's Word back to the accusing voice. He also focused on God's complete nourishment rather than a quickly devoured piece of bread. Jesus chose what was lasting and kingdom-valuable.

- The devil *unveiled the vast and beautiful Holy City*, then told Jesus to throw himself down (Matt. 4:6). Might Jesus have wanted to prove God's power? Might He have thought about all the doubters, the people who didn't believe, and wanted to prove Himself?

  The Way, the Truth, and the Life angle: Jesus kept His eyes on His mission. Our mission is to live full of faith, hope, and love, at all times and in all ways.

- Satan *displayed the kingdoms of the world* to Jesus. He offered them to Jesus, if only He would "bow down and worship" him (Matt. 4:9).

  The Way, the Truth, and the Life angle: Jesus replied to the devil, "You must worship the Lord your God." Sometimes we have to adamantly say no to a destructive relationship or a voice that is contrary to God's. We may need to say within our mind, *No, I do not accept that as truth*. We are not obligated to agree with everything people say. However, we may be wise to forgive if we feel hurt. Our aim should be to proceed with love.

What new angle might you need to consider? What kind of risk is involved in approaching it differently?

Some people consider risks like this:

1. *I'll look bad.* But let me assure you, God on you always looks good.
2. *I won't be taken care of; I'll be defenseless.* Did you notice Jesus's attack? It was God's perspective. Pick up the sword of the Spirit.
3. *Trials will ruin me.* Friends, we are not without power; a special arming comes when we do things God's way.
4. *People will think poorly of me.* People will think what they want to. Since when have you been able to control that? Much more important is what God thinks of you.

Certainly, new translations come with new obstructions we must learn to jump over.

Just recently, I saw things all wrong. I started blaming people I loved about things I'd heard through the grapevine of talking mouths. I interpreted the situation poorly. I misunderstood. I expected them to act a certain way. So much so I almost lost the relationships. Then I saw rightly. They weren't the problem, I was. I had been prideful. I began to see. My ears started to hear. I confessed my wrong and forgave. Love wanted to move out, in the form of me being humble.

> For the flesh desires what is contrary to the Spirit, and the Spirit what is contrary to the flesh. (Gal. 5:17)

The second we see past our flesh, we begin to see by the Spirit.

Our flesh lies, but God's truth never does.

Let's think about this concept as it pertains to our everyday lives.

If: You see your husband look up at you with frustration in his eyes, then put his hands on his hips.

You likely think: *Oh, great, he is angry at me again. I am so annoyed. I am not putting up with this.*

But what you don't know is: He just read a text from work saying he was being laid off.

God's truth: "Be sympathetic" (1 Pet. 3:8).

If: You see *that* truck parked in your driveway as you come from a walk and you scream repeatedly, "Move it!" because you figure the neighbor's workers are—once again—parking in your space (only to find it is the repair guy you called).

You likely think: *What is wrong with me? Why am I always a jerk? I can't do anything right.*

But what you don't know is: The guy was talking on his cell phone and couldn't even hear you. He only noticed you when you walked up.

God's truth: "Be compassionate" (1 Pet. 3:8).

If: You don't see a phone call, text, or email from your supposed BFF for weeks.

You likely think: *I am not good enough. I ruined the relationship. I am a bad friend. I can't keep friends. I am unworthy. I am a failure. I am abandoned. I messed up again! What did I do wrong?*

But what you don't know is: Her dad died and she flew to London on short notice to be with her family.

God's truth: "Love is patient" (1 Cor. 13:4).

If: You are talking with a friend at an event and you happen to see your common friend, Jane, across the room . . . and you just can't help yourself, so you sort of spill the beans and gossip about all the juicy details of her horror story at home.

You likely think: *I am bad. I am always messing up. I can't win/ do this. I am a loser. I deserve punishment. I hate myself. God hates me. I am unlikable. I can't forgive myself. I [fill in the blank].*

But what you don't know is: Grace is instantaneous; the second you say you're sorry, it's settled.

God's truth: "We do not have a high priest who is unable to empathize with our weaknesses" (Heb. 4:15).

If: You see that woman—the one with the yard like a botanical garden, the kids who belong in a Polo ad, the one who carries the charisma of Jackie O.

You likely think: *I am a loser. I am ugly. I am worthless. I am stuck. I need to be perfect. I am not enough. I need to try harder. I'll do more.*

But what you don't know is: She was once a model who got ridiculed for having acne. She can't let go of this overwhelming sense her face needs to be flawless or else no one will love her. She walks around wondering if people notice the scars.

God's truth: "Follow God's example, therefore, as dearly loved children and walk in the way of love, just as Christ loved us" (Eph. 5:1–2).

As I see it, the flesh speaks what it humanly sees; the Spirit speaks what God sees.

[Jesus said,] "But when he, the Spirit of truth, comes, he will guide you into all the truth. He will not speak on his own; he will speak only what he hears, and he will tell you what is yet to come." (John 16:13)

Wouldn't you love to more often know God's view so you don't agonize over yours?

His deep secrets?

"His Spirit searches out everything and *shows us God's deep secrets*" (1 Cor. 2:10 NLT, emphasis added).

His counsel?

"The Spirit searches all things [diligently], even [sounding and measuring] the [profound] depths of God [the divine counsels and things far beyond human understanding]" (1 Cor. 2:10 AMP).

His wonderful things?

"Now we have received, not the spirit of the world, but the [Holy] Spirit who is from God, so that we may know *and* understand the [wonderful] things freely given to us by God" (1 Cor. 2:12 AMP).

His life and power?

To "experience the love of Christ"? To be "complete with all the fullness of life and power that comes from God" (Eph. 3:19 NLT)?

The Spirit gives us God's inside view so we don't have to rely on ours.

I pray that the eyes of your heart may be enlightened in order that you may know the hope to which he has called you, the riches of his glorious inheritance in his holy people. (Eph. 1:18)

There is a grand hope to which we are each called. May we see, hear, and understand it. Why? So that through enlightened eyes we can step out from

1. staying stuck
2. repeating bad behavior
3. getting caught up in self-reproach
4. limiting the future
5. deflecting reality

6. losing faith
7. waning in joy
8. obstructing grace
9. distancing relationships
10. listening to lies

Rather than seeing apparent annoyances, by faith may we see God's unapparent reality at work to change everything.

> Now faith is confidence in what we hope for and assurance about what we do not see. (Heb. 11:1)

Point 4: Lessons and Keys You Can Daily Hold and Leverage

This morning I couldn't find my keys. Scratching my head, I was confused. I knew I'd tucked them into the elastic in my pants moments earlier. They weren't there.

I glanced in the bathroom. Not there. I eyeballed the kitchen. Gone. My eyes looked over the table. No go.

I always lose things. I tossed down the items balled up in my hands. *Thud.* My keys. They dropped before me plain as day.

Hmm . . . I was holding the key I needed all along. So often we are too. Available to us is the mind of Christ. A mind of truth.

Let's look at a few short stories so that when our thoughts get seemingly lost, we can find them, once again, through truth.

The Reading-between-the-Lines Story

Today my friend told another friend via text, "I love how you are so attentive to us." All I could think, when this happened, was, *She must be noticing how* inattentive *I am . . . how busyness has distracted me, how I'm not a good friend, how I'm not present in the many conversations, how I mess up.* I felt busted.

Lost Key

Say to yourself: *If I choose to believe people mean what they say, I can ditch the hours, days, and weeks of worry I subject myself to.*

The I-Hate-How-I-Look Story

The other day, I thought, *Yeah, if I got my hair looking less frizzy and more blonde, then I'd feel great when I walk outside.*

What if-then thinking paralyzes you? If I lose ten pounds, then my husband will love me? If I had bigger breasts, then I'd finally feel attractive? If I was 100 percent healthy, then I'd be loved?

Lost Key

Change the script. Say, "If God thinks _____ about me, then _____ is true." (Example: *If* God loves me as a daughter, *then* He thinks I am beautiful, even on my worst day.) Ask for the Holy Spirit's guidance, then write a list of all the positive if-thens that counteract your negative ones.

Refute: consider the lies and ask God for wisdom about the truth. Fight for the truth as if you were a lawyer. Make a case for it in your mind.

If-then thought example: *If I were rich, then I'd be happy.*

Rebuttal: if people who are richer are happier, then why would lottery winners say words like this: "I wish we had torn the ticket up," "I'd have been better off broke," "[People are] turning into vampires trying to suck the life out of me," and "My life was hijacked by the lottery."[1] Perhaps my faulty view of happiness is not the answer.

The Nuanced Story

While visiting friends, I looked at my husband and put on a sad face. He looked at me and gave me a thumbs-up. After spending time alone with each spouse, we were both getting a different story.

One spouse said life smelled as good as fresh-cut roses. The other said it stunk worse than week-old trash.

Lost Key

While people present us with their best, their reality is often far worse. People present image first and predicaments later.

What if we were to . . .

1. Consider: what we see in others is often not what we get.
2. Listen closely and attentively for the deeper story.
3. Reflect on this: what gold shines today likely resulted because someone endured the fire of yesterday. Affirm them on this.
4. Ask people about their story. Their heart. Their learnings. Their journey. So we can allow the Counselor, the Spirit, to reach in and touch the unseen areas of their life.
5. Consider: God might have put us in the path of this person for a reason, a learning, encouragement, and so forth.

The You're-So-Intense Story

Someone who noticed my personality called me "intense." This irritated the stink out of me, because who wants to be known as intense? Call me funny. Call me giving. Call me nice. But intense? I hated that word from the moment it was spoken. It was nothing near likable.

Lost Keys

1. Ask: Why do I let one person's could-be-wrong opinion of me supersede God's made-me-just-right declaration over me?
2. Consider: If the word *holy* means "set apart," why do I get so upset when my unique qualities actually set me apart? Isn't this how God uses people?

3. Observe: Just as there is variety at a convenience store, there is variety in our individual makeups. If we were all the same, we'd all sit on the shelf like a boring brand of *same*. The world needs what we offer; it needs the creative, wild, soft, energetic, quiet, or intense version of us! There is no measure in us that goes un- or underutilized when we are led by God.

Point 5: Thirty-Second Practices That Deliver Peace

To detach from the world and attach to God leads to understanding. But, as we all know, things happen fast. With this, we need to be able to reangle our mind quickly back to truth. Here are some ideas to help you to gain objectivity in the face of adversity.

1. Ask God how He sees you. Write it down.
2. Choose to get out from under condemnation by telling yourself, "There is now no condemnation for those who are in Christ Jesus" (Rom. 8:1).
3. Seek out the things God might see. Internally comment on these in hard situations.
4. Remember: opinions are subjective interpretations not belonging to God.
5. Avoid talking to yourself like Judge Judy, and instead remember Jesus makes up the jury.
6. Be less concerned with deciding success/failure and more concerned with enjoying God in the moment of what He is doing, as you believe He'll bring a good end.
7. Remind yourself:
   - I can stop letting others define my worth, because God does.

- I have the freedom to choose flesh- or Spirit-thinking.
- I can close the door on criticisms, judgments, and proclamations that don't align with God's Word.
- I can find peace in letting God take care of the people I can't.
- I am able to reject false truth masquerading as God's.
- I can say no and still feel okay with myself.
- I am not beholden to others and still remain beloved by God.
- I am not a victim because others hurt me; I am a victor because Christ loves me.

8. Lay your problems up against the size of your God. Read some verses from Job 38–39.

9. Live a "no rewind" mentality. Only play out life moving forward. No dwelling on the past.

10. Add the word "but" to your negative outlooks. Example: I am tired today, *but* God will renew my strength.

11. Repeat in your mind, *God's love will go forth from me, as I relate to [insert the person you're standing before]*. Note: this doesn't mean you soak in all their problems, issues, and fears; it means you love from the place of the already-saturated fullness, the complete love of Jesus within you.

<<< IMPLEMENT >>> "1 Quick-Tip Bound to Keep You Extremely Objective." Find it at www.iambattleready.com.

Bad TRANSLATIONS = Big PROBLEMS

⚜

HAVE A Buffet MIND-SET

⚜

SEE THE Way, THE Truth, AND

THE Life ANGLE

⚜

USE THE WORDS

And AND But

A MIND TO CONQUER

It's not necessarily what happened that hurts most but how we keep retranslating it, day after day, year after year, to no end.

PRAY

Father, I have a feeling there is so much of You I cannot see. Give me Your eyes to see and Your ears to hear. Open up to me the fullness of You and the vastness of Your kingdom. I want to see others as You see them. I want to love others as You love. I want to speak as You speak. Teach me how to be kind to myself and to let the overflow of my heart pour out on the world. In Jesus's name. Amen.

WRITE THREE THINGS YOU'RE THANKFUL FOR

1. _____

2. _____

3. _____

ENTER YOUR MIND

Are you a perfectionist?

Perfectionists believe they should be perfect—no hesitations, deviations, or inconsistencies. They are super-sensitive to imperfection, failing, and weakness. They believe their acceptance and lovability is a function of never making mistakes. And they don't know the meaning of "good enough."[2]

Perfectionists often have *conditional self-esteem:* They like themselves when they are on top and *dislike* themselves when things don't go their way. Can you learn to like yourself even when you

159

are not doing well? Focus on inner qualities like your character, sincerity, or good values, rather than just on what grades you get, how much you get paid, or how many people like you.[3]

EXAMINE YOUR STORY

1. What assumptions have you placed on people? Circumstances? Issues? How have these hurt you?

2. How might you have translated them all wrong? What other causes might there be? How could you see the good? Why might people have acted as they did?

3. What judgments might God be calling you to leave behind? In what ways are you critical, overbearing, or hard-hitting?

4. In the case of your worst behavior, how does God treat you? (Refer to Psalm 103:8.)

5. What do you see in yourself (qualities, appearances, attitudes) that God might see differently? Make a list. Write what you see and what God likely sees (use Scripture).

6. Imagine God writing a note to you about His mercy and grace. Pray and ask Him to lead you. Then write down what He would say. Receive all the forgiveness and restoration He has for you.

EXPLORE WITH GROUP STUDY

1. What did you learn from your personal study time?

2. What kind of buffet mentality can you spread before yourself as you consider mind change? What can you remind yourself of?

3. How could seeing like God sees change so much in your life? In others' lives?

4. With emotional and physical safety boundaries, how could you move out to love the most difficult person in your life?

What would this look like practically? How could you remind yourself to do this in the heat of difficult moments?

5. How have you seen God advance His kingdom mission (love, peace, hope) in the face of a past trial? How has He been faithful?

6. Pick a problem situation. Reframe it from the Way, the Truth, and the Life angle.

7. Do you remember a time or story when love changed a person's demeanor, actions, or life? Share with the group.

8. Encourage each other. Take a moment to notice what is good in each other (as God would see it) and share it within the group.

A CHRIST-CENTERED PRINCIPLE
GOD BLESSES

Objectivity founded in God's wisdom

Blessed are those who find wisdom, those who gain understanding, for she is more profitable than silver and yields better returns than gold. (Prov. 3:13–14)

Intermission Two

A Minding Grace Note

Dear Reader,

I find law-keeping not to be freedom but bondage. If you're starting to feel you need to follow this book to the letter of the law, then perhaps it's wise I remind you of Love. Love came on account of you and poured out His life, His blood. Love had His body broken so yours could be restored forever. Love let go of your every past wrong and turned them right in His sight. Love rose again and filled you with His Spirit. Love sees you. Love empowers you. Love fills you to the complete measure of God, making you look like Christ. When you're overwhelmed by the never-able-to-be-fulfilled law, lean back on the always-present, never-failing love of Christ. It will lead you home.

Love,
Kelly

And I pray that you, being rooted and established in love, may have power, together with all the Lord's holy people, to grasp how wide and long and high and deep is the love of Christ, and to know this love that surpasses knowledge—that you may be filled to the measure of all the fullness of God. (Eph. 3:17–19)

*Success Is as Simple as Letting God
Help You Back Up, Again and Again*

(Bounce-Back Ability)

> Failure is just part of the process, and it's not just okay;
> it's better than okay. God doesn't want failure to shut
> us down. God didn't make it a three-strikes-and-you're-
> out sort of thing. It's more about how God helps us
> dust ourselves off so we can swing for the fences again.
> And all of this without keeping a meticulous record of
> our screw-ups.
>
> Bob Goff, *Love Does*

Point 1: Thoughts That Make You Hit Rock Bottom

Just recently, I sent out a cruddy blog post. This morning I woke,
rubbed my eyes, and read an email telling me how I had basically
done a pretty good job until the last line, where I pretty much
botched it. I agreed with her. I had ended that blog post with the
words, "Watch out, God just might pull through."

God never *might* pull through. He always *does* pull through.

My slip of mind was subconscious, but the reality was stark. I
wasn't believing what I pretended to believe.

165

Taking a step back, I considered my thoughts of late:

* I am moving in two weeks and have no home.
* Everything is *so* expensive.
* Selling half my furniture is hard, and getting a smaller place feels hard.
* I've already moved five times in four years.
* I don't know what to do.
* I need to write this book.
* I am all alone.
* I've got to sell this very couch I'm sitting on, yet it has my book notes spread out on it like an encyclopedia of notecards. And I have nowhere else to write and it's my only comfortable seat in the house and there's no time to do anything and everything is going to topple down and I am not a good mom or a good wife and I am really not sure about anything I am doing. . . .

While my mind was supposed to

think good,
think true, and
think right about me, my people, and my problems,

I was only thinking

mean things about me,
cruel thoughts toward my family,
and hopeless thoughts toward my problems.

Everyone is against me. Everything is against me. There's no way. I'm in a bind this time. No one can help me. I am in for it now. Everyone is frustrating. I want to run away.
Ever noticed? Our mind subtly and unnoticeably shifts away from truth little by little.

166

One day we're on fire for Jesus, the next we can't pick up our Bible. One day we're encouraging someone in Christ, a week later we're hiding from them in shame. One day we rise up strong in prayer, a month later we're frozen in chill-out mode. Or destroyed by doubt. Or wrecked by uncertainty. Or shifted by circumstances.

Our mind tracks subtly; we hardly notice its descent.

Until the day comes when we go over the "Cliff of (Seemingly) No Return." There we're nearly convinced we lost God, or He lost us. We're about to be ruined or will never be the same. We are hated by God or others. We are broken or irreparable.

We didn't reach this place because of one thing or another but because of many unnoticeable, un-paid-attention-to things that added up over time. It was subtle.

Marketers know how our mind doesn't recognize subtle shifts. They have established a point of "just noticeable difference." Here, we don't notice they put less chips in our bag than before. We just munch away like nothing happened. But something did happen. And something does happen in our mind, even if we don't notice it. Small shifts add up. Until one day we slam our face on the rocks.

Don't discount the small grievances, pent-up annoyances, or mounting irritations in your life.

A leak starts small, but left unaddressed it turns into a raging downpour of discouragement. Or a mouth that shoots off at a husband. Or a bombastic display of tears at the kitchen counter. Or a sense of purposelessness or lostness.

Small, negative mind shifts construct ruts—then you fall into them.

Where are you at today? Where do you feel discouraged? Doubtful? Disappointed? Alone? Abandoned? Here are six warning signs you may be approaching the cliff of (seemingly) no return:

1. You regret you are regretting. You hate yourself for what you did. You can't make up for the past.

Example thoughts: *I shouldn't have moved. I picked the wrong school for my kids. I am always making a mountain out of a molehill. I never should have married him. I knew this wasn't the right ___.*

2. You don't know how to embrace change. You liked what was and are having a hard time facing the reality of what is coming or what is different.

Example thoughts: *I don't know what to do if I don't get that job. I can't think what it'll be like without kids around. I don't know how to begin. I can see a new season coming, but I like where I am. I am going to have to tackle a different life, but it feels painful. I must have what I had.*

3. You feel like the world's punching bag. It feels the world is pushing you around, telling you what to do. It is acting on you. You feel out of control.

Example thoughts: *They are mean women. I am always left out. I can't ever win. Her face said it all. Bad things always happen to me. I never present myself right. I am jaded. He always acts indifferent. God isn't taking care of me.*

4. You can't forgive yourself. You've already put yourself in the rut because you feel so torn up inside about what you did.

Example thoughts: *I am so bad. I am not godly. I am not good. God must be angry at me. I can't imagine He'd ever love me. I need an improvement plan. I need to shape up or ship out. I'd better start being thankful or else something bad will happen.*

5. You keep missing what you hope for. You've tried so hard and failed. You can't keep trying. It is taking too long.

Example thoughts: *He's not improving. I'll never have a nice house, car, or clothes. I never get chosen. I keep getting a bad bill of health. We're not getting that opportunity. I never have enough money. I'll be infertile forever. I'll never be young and pretty again. I give up.*

6. You are triggered. A resurfacing feeling of inadequacy or insecurity triggers your thoughts. Or a person constantly triggers you by their actions. It is a stimulus-reaction kind of thing. Something acts on you; you react.

Example thoughts: *I am selfish. I am untrustworthy. I am guilty. I am bad. I am ashamed. I am not honest. I am stupid. I am unchangeable. I am damaged goods. I am unlovable and cannot love. I am unworthy. They are bad. They are mean.*

Monitor these things closely.

Point 2: Your CliffsNotes Version of Life

In my house, we have a faulty fire alarm. At the first scent of bacon the thing is all *Bleep! Bleep! Bleep!* We preheat the oven: *Bleep! Bleep! Bleep!* We wake up at 5 a.m., get the oven going, and it hits us like a drill sergeant: *Bleep! Bleep! Bleep! Wake up! Get on it!*

At first I hated it. And we all panicked. My husband and I would sprint over with blankets. We'd fan that thing like it was the prince of Egypt. It took forever to shut off.

Now, though, I've begun to like that alarm.

Why? Because I've begun to see it for what it represents: a shortcut to good thinking. Rather than inadvertently stepping over the edge of the cliff, I let it sound in my mind. And it saves me.

It screams, "Watch it! Watch it! Watch it!" Watch it—you are on the verge of criticizing that woman in your head rather than loving her. Watch it—you are counting all your losses rather than all the blessings you've been given. Watch it—all these domino-like issues (first the car dent, then your kids' attitudes, followed by a trip to the hospital) are about to send your mind overboard.

Having an alarm sound in your mind, while annoying, is life-saving. It diverts disaster before it can blow. I like that alarm now.

A mind alarm catches the "just noticeable difference" and sees it for what it is.

- It recognizes what is coming (example: tension and anxiety when leaving the house for school).
- It takes a moment to observe what is behind it (example: no time to let the kids play).
- It considers how to handle things differently (example: start the morning earlier).

What alarm do you need to set up in order to keep standing tall and avoid your fall? What do you need to talk to God about? Confess? Rethink?

Point 3: Resilient People Remember These Ten Secrets of Resiliency

Every victor falls. Victorious warriors are simply those who choose to get back up again, no matter the cost or . . . *even though [fill in your own trauma here]*. They do this because they understand the normal cycle of progress goes something like this:

1. You'll try your best.
2. You'll mess up, fall down, think bad, do bad, and/or act stupid.
3. You'll try to do other things to fix things.
4. You'll try and fail again.
5. Here, this doesn't mean God isn't growing you . . .
6. Or transforming you . . .
7. Or that He isn't proud of you or guiding you.
8. It means you are human.
9. And you can always step back out of your sorry pit through the freeing and forgiving love of Jesus Christ that marks you pure and holy.

They also know these ten secrets of resiliency:

1. There are cliff pushers, so push them back. Don't let rejection, comparison, people pleasing, or sadness push you over the edge. Let God's truth push them back. Pray blessings over those who persecute you. Remember how God sees you.

2. You can rally your heart. Acknowledge your pain and speak to it with words of encouragement and truth, just like you believe God would if He were before you.

3. Know trials will come. Through the worst of times, God is providing wisdom that'll stand the test of time.

4. You can always be a blessing, even when going through a time of testing. Praise God for the goodness of who He is and what He has given you in your life. Thank Him.

5. Friends are friends for a reason. As iron sharpens iron, so people sharpen people (Prov. 27:17).

6. Relaxation will replenish you. God fights battles. He fights while you feel you're doing nothing—in your silence, in your periods of rest, and through your prayers. God reigns over every battle. He defeated death. How much more can He defeat for you?

7. Asking why helps. Keep asking yourself why until you land at your underlying issue. *Why do I feel angry?* Because I am left behind by my friends. *Why am I left behind by my friends?* Maybe because I always tell them I can't hang out. *Why do I tell them I can't hang out?* Because I am scared of being rejected. Bring this to God and bring His truth to your underlying issue.

8. The truth is you're moving from glory to glory. Yesterday, I pulled out a four-year-old journal of mine. Wow, was I mean to myself! I chastised my efforts. I hated how I was. I've come a long way. But I never would have noticed. We often don't. Know this: you've come further than you give yourself credit for. Our good change can be just as gradual as our bad.

9. Jesus suffered too, but that didn't stop Him. We all suffer. Another person's suffering doesn't negate yours. Jesus suffered, but He never quit. The price of His calling was too high. So is ours. Never give up, no matter how hard it is.

10. Do "space and grace." When my husband and I get in a tiff or feel frustrated, one of us may throw out, "I need space and grace." This means we need space to process and grace for our mind-set that is lagging behind. The other person knows to love like Christ, to give leeway to offenses, and to pray. We also need to offer space and grace to our own hearts. Sometimes you need room to make room to let God revive you.

Falling and getting back up again is not a fault, it is a strength. A massive one. One that there is no shame in. In fact, I am a believer in new starts—often. We don't have to wait until the New Year to do a new thing. Right now is your new day that begins your new year. You don't need a special calendar date. Just start. Start here:

Today, on (insert the date here), I will: _____.

Then, if you fall, start the pledge all over again, with no shame. Your new angle is excitement because you now have gained new learning to see things through. You have more ammo to win with.

Begin again:

Today, on (insert the date here), I will: _____.

Point 4: Foundational Truths That *Always* Put You Back on Safe Ground

Remember Jesus's testing? The devil said to Jesus, as He stood on a cliff, "If you are the Son of God, throw yourself down from here" (Luke 4:9).

The devil loves to say to us, *Prove yourself.*

Prove you can handle life, your problems, your issues, your children, your Christian walk, your funk, your marriage, your finances, your faith, your beliefs. Prove you're a self-sufficient woman. Prove you are a good mom. Show. Me. Your. Stuff.

So we painstakingly try to "prove" ourselves. We try to muscle up control, care, justice, peace, progress, hope, strength, or will-power on our own. But what inevitably happens is, in the name of self-sufficiency, we get stunted by our deficiencies.

And then we're straight-up angry. Angry because all our little tests to prove we're valuable, smart, able, and wise . . . didn't work. *Where were You, God? Why didn't You show up?*

Jesus replied to the devil, "Do not put the Lord your God to the test" (Luke 4:12).

Where is your flesh putting the power of God to the test? Where, by your might, are you trying to improve yourself and outmuscle God? Running against the wind?

While Jesus could have chosen "to prove" Himself and tasered the enemy right there and then; while He could have bolted him with lightning; while He could have jumped off the cliff and been caught by God—He didn't. He hardly spoke. Nearly three years later, He took his last breath and died.

The only thing Jesus proved is that He ultimately trusted the Father, even during hardship. Resiliency is knowing whose you are so you don't fall into the "proving" trap that only leaves you tired, weary, and all busted up.

We are pressed on every side by troubles, but we are not crushed. We are perplexed, but not driven to despair. We are hunted down, but never abandoned by God. (2 Cor. 4:8–9 NLT)

God is not abandoning you, even if it feels like you are doing nothing.

Why?

BANNER of LOVE

SWORD of the SPIRIT

GOD'S ANGEL ARMIES

SHIELD of FAITH

BELT of TRUTH

CHRIST'S SOLID ROCK FOUNDATION

A woman armed with the power and protection of God can't easily be taken down.

"The LORD will fight for you; you need only to be still" (Exod. 14:14).

"The battle is not yours, but God's" (2 Chron. 20:15).

"[God] will instruct you and teach you in the way you should go; [He] will counsel you with [His] loving eye on you" (Ps. 32:8).

Whatever you face, it doesn't matter. Like what happened in Acts, your enemies will start to say things like, "But if she is of God, you will not be able to stop her. You may even find yourself fighting against God" (see Acts 5:39).

Resiliency knows the G.R.A.C.E. of Jesus is more than enough. It remembers: Jesus reigns. He is my victor. The overcomer of my impossible. Strength for my last leg. Life when I have none. The Word when I'm defenseless. My power perfected in weakness. My armor dispersing the enemy. My shield that diverts bullets. My deflector who deadens arrows. My sword of the Spirit who slays. Lion. Lamb. Love. Releaser of the angel armies.

Jesus is not dead. He is alive. He's actively working in my life. Nothing can stop His power.

"This I declare about the LORD: He alone is my refuge, my place of safety; he is my God, and I trust him" (Ps. 91:2 NLT).

Speaking these things reloads your quiver with power. His strength supernaturally recharges yours. This is bounce-back ability.

 <<<DISCOVER >>> "5 Proven Ways to Develop Perseverance" at www.iambattleready.com.

Remember

THE JUST-NOTICEABLE DIFFERENCE

Sound AN ALARM

Fail, THEN *Get Up* AGAIN

Die TO SELF TO SEE JESUS *Rise*

THE *Battle* IS *God's*

A MIND TO CONQUER

If you let go of what you can't change,
you'll find yourself free to change.

PRAY

Dear God, we aren't perfect, but You are. We aren't sure of our way, but You know our way. Help us to let go of what is holding us back and to find out You are holding us. The time for us to move ahead is now. You have great things to do with our lives and with the lives of others. We submit our plans to You. In Jesus's name. Amen.

WRITE THREE THINGS YOU'RE THANKFUL FOR

1. _____

2. _____

3. _____

ENTER YOUR MIND

Psychologist Melanie Greenberg noted,

Denying the reality of a bad situation, or avoiding thinking about it at all, makes it worse—or keeps you stuck when you could be working on solving the problem. Awareness is the first step to change. Be willing to face the problem, but don't dwell on it 24 hours a day. This will just make you feel worse. Think about it enough to understand what you feel and the best way to respond, then focus on something more positive. Research suggests that avoiding thinking about or dealing with problems actually creates *more* stressors, a phenomenon known as "stress generation." For example, if you don't open the envelopes with your bills, you will end up getting calls from collection agencies.[1]

EXAMINE YOUR STORY

1. What is the truth of your difficult situation?

2. What rejection, isolation, or discouragement has crept up on you? What dreams feel lost? What irritants keep coming at you?

3. How have you taken on a victim mentality? What are you doing to yourself?

4. Which of the six warning signs do you tend not to heed? Why?

EXPLORE WITH GROUP STUDY

1. What did you learn from your personal study time?

2. Share a time when your mind went over a cliff. How did you learn to bounce back after that?

3. *Grit* means courage, resolve, and strength of character. What does a person who has grit look like in everyday life? What practices do you imagine them using to rise up?

4. Which of the ten secrets of resiliency do you believe could make the biggest difference in your life? How could it change your situation? Why?

5. Do you know what it is to be Christ's? It means the following statements are true:

   • I am holy.

   • I am blameless in Christ Jesus.

   • I am restored by Christ.

   • I am covered by the love of Jesus.

   Which of these brings your heart the greatest relief? What might it mean for you to believe it? How can you apply these words to your life?

6. How has God fought your battles in the past? How have you seen Him as victor?

7. What Bible verses also encourage you to not give up? Discuss them.

A CHRIST-CENTERED PRINCIPLE
GOD BLESSES

Bounce-back ability, or resiliency, in trials

Blessed is the one who perseveres under trial because, having stood the test, that person will receive the crown of life that the Lord has promised to those who love him. (James 1:12)

Warrior Mind-Set Eight

Throw the Junk Away to Find the Gem

(Simplicity)

If the devil cannot make us bad, he will make us busy.

Anonymous

Point 1: The Constant Battle You Fear You'll Never Win

I was eager to "reconnect." For far too long, my husband and I had been passing like shadows in the night.

I'd planned our night to perfection: the babysitter already knew what to do with the kids, the restaurant was set to be spectacular, and the conversation points were mostly outlined in my head.

I'm sure I imagined it all playing out. Us smiling at each other over a candlelit dessert. The love rekindled. The feeling as we held hands. The eager discussion about "life."

It would be a flawless night. So would be my outfit. Flawless. It would be one that would subliminally tell my husband: *You matter. I want to be beautiful for you.* He'd be proud of me. He'd love spending time with me.

But as I stood in my closet, running through every option, no outfit was right. Many were wrinkled. Some had "shrunk in the dryer." Others looked old.

I didn't feel like wearing a dress. My favorite jeans were missing. The white pants didn't sit right. The silk top was missing. The blue skirt was still in the washing machine. The panic was rising. I was getting frustrated. *Why don't things work out for me? Why is it so difficult?*

Pushing aside mounds of clothes, I tried to climb under my busting-at-the-seams racks to find some semblance of what I needed. I could hardly make my way in. I had all this stuff—stuff I didn't even like. Stuff that was stressing me out. Somehow, I had everything yet nothing at the same time.

Hunched, I moved under and through it all like a grunting, salivating bear seeking dinner. That is—until I stepped on it, a spear or something like that . . . *Yee-owww!*

A belt of my husband's with the spoke sticking up. *Ouch! Ouch! Ouch!*

My husband arrived during the moment of my agony to say, "I can't wait for tonight."

I grunted in disgust, or something to that effect, and shook his hand off my shoulder. He walked away. I lost the war.

The whole night was ruined, all thanks to my overstuffed closet.

My everything left me with nothing. And isn't this emblematic of our lives? We can't keep up with "meaning" because we are managing everything. We can't keep our cool because we feel hot with frustration about all we have to do. We hate that we have so much, yet we want it all. Something is wrong here.

Our world stuff is stealing the heart-replenishing soul stuff we most crave.

In what ways are you overstuffing? Are you overstuffing your:

- Emotions with others' worries?
- Week with one thousand activities?

- Text message inbox with random chatter/gossip/complaining?
- Closet and home with impromptu purchases?
- Mind with personal grievances?
- Spirit with nighttime news?
- Schedule with activities that leave you tense, jealous, or afraid?
- Body with the sense you have to do everything?
- Day with work that leaves you unfulfilled, angry, or bitter?
- Thoughts that demand you reach your every expectation of yourself?
- Friendships in such a way that you are friendly to everyone and loving to no one?
- Heart with others' opinions, doubts, fears, regrets, or burdens?
- Peace with dinging distractions, notifications, and pop-ups?

To overstuff is usually to consider God underrated. Not because you don't love Him but because you want everything else too. Then *all that* ends up clouding your view.

In addition, overstuffing tends to:

- Paralyze people in indecision.
- Confuse focus.
- Diminish wisdom.
- Create a sense of lack.
- Increase dissatisfaction.
- Bury what is most important.
- Set up an impossible race to win.
- Foster an identity built on appearances, image, and self-importance.
- Mute the voice of God.

Not only this, it rips soul intimacy away. You can't easily be listening to your son, your friend, or your husband when you're running ten feet ahead in order to keep the whole moving-in-tandem circus going. Or when you're tapping at your phone the 2,617 times an average person does a day.[1]

But we do it because we've always done it. And because everyone else is doing it. So we say, *More clothes! More things to do! More activities! More friends! More Facebook! More beauty products! More shoes! More vacations! More stuff!*

And we get our "more," while at home we feel discontented.

Without room to understand God's best, we settle for the world's average.

We give in to a fast-food life . . . with texts arriving by the dozen . . . an endless list of to-dos and house-upkeep items. . . a hundred and one activities the family needs to attend to . . . an online cart full of clothes. . . a pile of bills on the counter . . . dreams unaddressed . . . soul empty . . . relationships on edge . . . heart guarded . . . and life empty.

I should know. I've lived in subjection to this demanding lifestyle that requires perfect execution. I've given in to the winds of the world.

But those winds get brutal. For instance, gross domestic product has doubled in the last thirty years and people are less happy.[2] We have more choices than ever, but studies prove we're frozen in inaction and indecision, buying less. Somehow we got "the everything" we never wanted.[3]

And we hate it. We continually purchase more anxiety, worry, and fear. We know we can't effectively manage it all. Our stuff cripples us. Add this to the fast-moving targets of celebrity fashion and home decorating and we have more pressure on our shoulders. Buzzing at our side is our cell phone that drives us nuts. Almost every day, we live constantly distracted. To make matters worse, even the presence of our turned-off phone distracts us or impairs our brain.[4] Why do we do this to ourselves?

Point 2: Self-Assessment: Learn Why You Struggle
to Follow Jesus

Imagine you hear this: "Come, follow Me."

It sounds like a great idea! You know this guy; He brings people to good places—peace, hope, and love places. You've gone with Him before. So you like the idea. You want to go, except for one thing: you are weighed down. Like a sinking rock.

You're holding seven loaded grocery bags. Their handles dig deep. In fact, you're probably losing all circulation in your hand. And we've only spoken of the left side. Your right hand is holding your ten-pound daily planner full of life activities (and stuffed-in paperwork, receipts, and notes). You try to balance it. And this is not to speak of your back, on which you carry a book bag loaded with everyone's needs, your world news burdens, and your friends' issues. Your mind travels 101 miles an hour trying to keep up with the 101 things you should have done yesterday. Your phone keeps buzzing too.

As much as you want to, you can't follow *this guy*. You have things to do. And you can hardly breathe.

So when He invites you to peace, you just tell Him, "There's no room for all that. I can't walk away from all the obligations, promises, and commitments I've made."

And so He walks away.

And you just go on with your five-minute Bible study, occasional prayer, and church on Sunday, and call it a day. Then a week. Then a month. Then your life. That you hate.

"Come, follow Me," Jesus says.

Will we?

Maybe you remember the one man who approached Jesus, saying, "Good teacher, what must I do to inherit eternal life?" (Mark 10:17).

Jesus said, "One thing you lack. Go, sell everything you have and give to the poor, and you will have treasure in heaven. Then come, follow me" (Mark 10:21).

185

Might he have thought . . .

Who, me?
I've got all this stuff going on.
I've got too much to manage.
Everyone else is doing what I am doing.
You can't really mean—me?

"At this the man's face fell, and he went away sad, for he had many possessions" (Mark 10:22 NLT).

You know, we can easily live with good intentions and no vision because our pile of stuff blocks our view. Or we can clear that stuff away and pursue peace. And follow Him, no matter the sacrifice.

Which will you choose?

"Here I am! I stand at the door and knock. If anyone hears my voice and opens the door, I will come in and eat with that person, and they with me" (Rev. 3:20).

You are face-to-face with a God who wants to meet you. Who wants to love away the worries and wreckage that have come from your fast-paced life. From your life that makes you say:

"God, why do You give me so much?"
"God, why is it so hard?"
"God, don't You see all I'm doing for You?"
"God, why don't You replenish me?"
"God, why am I so overwhelmed?"
"God, I am angry at You; You don't help me."

Jesus never told his daughters to pick up their purses and to carry it all. He said, "Take my yoke upon you and learn from me, for I am gentle and humble in heart, and you will find rest for your souls" (Matt. 11:29).

Jesus wants to lead us to rest for our souls. May our riches never hold us back from His peace-filled, soul-settling riches. What sadness that would bring.

"For what will it profit a man if he gains the whole world and forfeits his soul?" (Matt. 16:26 ESV).

How do you forfeit soul rest, God's invitations, life, peace, and joy because you can't see over the crazy, maniacal life you've set up for yourself?

- ☐ You give in, saying yes, when you really should consider your answer. You are afraid to let people down.
- ☐ You listen to advice-giving friends before listening to God. They make you question your approach or your ability to get out of a situation.
- ☐ You find your surroundings distracting; your kitchen is such a mess you feel out of control.
- ☐ Text messages hit you every minute, distracting you from being present.
- ☐ Your schedule is so packed, it no longer has room for your heart to beat.
- ☐ Facebook continually feels like it is a soul-suck.
- ☐ People's expectations are mounting on you like paperwork on an office desk.
- ☐ All your commitments are catching up with you, and you don't know how to manage them.
- ☐ You never find time to be alone or to catch a sunset.
- ☐ Bills pile up, and every time you look at them you feel the weight of it all hit.
- ☐ Distractions tackle you in such a way that you can't think or move forward.
- ☐ Your DVR pulls you onto the couch of complacency and you can't get up.

- You can't stop thinking about impending dangers or how you should start a 401(k).
- You are defensive rather than proactive with life's happenings.
- You continually focus on the urgent rather than what your heart needs most.
- You have to keep up with email to feel on top of the world.
- You are afraid to make a decision because you fear you'll let people down.
- Other: ____

What did you learn about yourself? What do you gain by doing these things? What do you lose? Record your answers in the Examine Your Story section.

Point 3: What Looks Stupid to the World May Look Brilliant to God

I want to tell you about a man who must've really understood what it was like to walk a day in a modern woman's shoes. His world demanded things of him. People wanted him to do life a certain way. There was a culture to keep up with. There were things he was supposed to do.

This man, like us, could have thought . . .

I must appear a certain way.

I have to keep up.

I'll never succeed if I don't adopt the same mentality.

He also could have figured that in this kingdom, the kingdom of Babylon, there was only one way to do things: Babylon's way. The king's way or the highway. The man was Daniel. Daniel had been captured by a new world and immersed in a place that did *not* do things God's way.

For Daniel, going against this order was a giant risk.

But Daniel was determined not to defile himself by eating the food and wine given to them by the king. He asked the chief of staff for permission not to eat these unacceptable foods. (Dan. 1:8 NLT)

Daniel knew he needed to do things God's way.

Three times a day [Daniel] got down on his knees and prayed, giving thanks to his God, just as he had done before. (6:10)

Daniel not only prayed but he fasted, trusted, and stayed with God. He did this even though the well-fed men could beat him and cost him his life.

Daniel answered, ". . . My God sent his angel, and he shut the mouths of the lions. They have not hurt me, because I was found innocent in his sight." (vv. 21–22)

Daniel took the complicated and uncomplicated it. He followed through with simple acts of devotion and didn't let all the commotion deter him.

We can do the same. Do you know how? By saying: love first.

First, I love God.

First, I love others as myself.

This uncomplicates the complicated. We focus on what matters. And God takes care of us.

Look at how God provided for Daniel.

- Daniel got interpretation and understanding from God about the king's dreams.
- Daniel was blessed by God, who allowed him and his men to be "ten times better than all the magicians and enchanters in his whole kingdom" (Dan. 1:20).
- Daniel ruled over all the Babylonian wise men.
- Daniel was lavished with many gifts (Dan. 2:48).

- Daniel saw an angel in his moment of need.
- Daniel was miraculously rescued when shoved into a lions' den—he was saved by the hand of God.
- Daniel was noted by God for his righteousness (Ezek. 14:14).
- Daniel was chosen by God as a prophet. He was honored in a way that allowed him to deliver key prophecies and messages to many, including us.

If you lost what's overwhelming, distracting and demanding, how might you gain the life you always wanted?

For whoever wants to save their life will lose it, but whoever loses their life for me will find it. (Matt. 16:25)

Point 4: A List of Ten Things You Need to Stop Doing ASAP

A short while ago, I slowed my car way down—to about the speed limit. I wanted to see the ocean out the passenger side window. I wanted to see the birds flying above with all their swoops and woops. I wanted to check out the sun and how it kind of peeked out from behind a cloud but was also shining far and wide. I wanted to soak. Just soak it all in.

So when a car started to tailgate me and wouldn't stop, I got angry. He was messing me up. He was impacting my moment. He was causing me tension.

But then it occurred to me . . .

I don't have to let others push me when I don't want them to.

I don't have to rush when God whispers, "Slow down."

I don't have to miss the moment because the world moves at a different pace.

I don't have to heap on things to do because I figure I "have to."

I don't have to respond to immediacy.

I don't have to miss the moment.

I don't have to lose what I really want.

I don't have to rush, fear, or appease the world.

People can't stomp on my invitation unless I give them permission to.

What or who is tailgating you in such a way, there's a chance the beauty of God might be stolen from your day?

Stop and Start

Change is as simple as stopping one thing and starting another. So, let's start there.

The *stops*:

1. **Stop putting that "one more thing to do" first and foremost.**

   There will always be one more email to answer, one more cabinet to organize, one more check to write, and one more thing that needs to get handled. These things distract you from the One Thing.

2. **Stop ditching rest to do more.**

   You aren't unloved or unwanted if you don't have a full calendar of activities. You can handle the quiet. There is heart-work and delayering God wants to do in you, through rest. Go there with Him.

3. **Stop living with so much stuff.**

   I can't write with a messy desk. My mind gets distracted, so I declutter it. Our life also doesn't work well with the mess of social media jealousy, Pinterest envy, flurry of activity, or constant anxiety all around. Where do you need to declutter?

4. **Stop running around like a chicken with its head cut off as you put out every fire.**

   The dishes, the screams, the crumb-laden floors, and the rapid-fire texts will always be there. But what won't be there are the moments. Many of the smiles, the laughs, the games, the vacations with family—those pass, only to become memories.

Don't constantly address the urgent only to neglect the important moments (the cuddles with the baby, a mind that is listening, a heart to understand. . .). It is our momentary decisions that matter greatly.

5. **Stop constantly multitasking.**

The book *The 4 Disciplines of Execution* states it well: "Improving our ability to multitask actually hampers our ability to think deeply and creatively . . . the more you multitask the less deliberative you become; the less you are able to think."[5]

Just because we women can do everything doesn't mean we should. Trying to do everything all at the same time usually leaves us with stuff strewn all over the kitchen, a baby crying in one ear, a friend chattering over the phone in the other, and a pot boiling over. Doesn't sound like fun to me.

6. **Stop being so "same" you miss your unique goal.**

Often, we want to be the cookie-cutter copy of the perfect image. What a waste. God didn't make us all identical; He made us each totally different. For a reason.

What a bore if every shell was the same, every cloud was a perfect circle, every beach was the same shade of white, or every sunset was only red. You are *you* because you have unique value to add to the world. Embrace your difference, your uniqueness.

Start by asking yourself these questions:

- *What do I love to do?*
- *What qualities show God's best in me?*
- *What activities compel me?*
- *What kind of moments bring me joy?*
- *What do I love about me?*

7. **Stop being laser-focused on what you cannot change.**

   What you can't touch, you can't change. You can't change people's emotions, requests, requirements, reactions, well-being, goals, opinions, desires, or issues. You can let God change you.

   Funny enough, it's the change in us that usually ends up effecting change in others and in the world.

8. **Stop operating from a place of "I really should . . ."**

   I really should act nicer to my kids. I really should save money. I really should work out.

   My stomach churns at this kind of talk. While it seems good and noble at face value, words like this cloak negativity under the guise of an "I'll fix myself" mind-set. They're self-inflicted torture. Change your "should" to a "would." Make it a prayer: *God, would You help me?* And stop beating yourself up. No one ever got well by banging their head against a wall.

9. **Stop carrying around offenses.**

   If you let go of that second of injury that's beat you up for years, what freedom might you experience?

10. **Stop letting the world define your "wins."**

    You win when Jesus's love wins. That's the only time. It's not when you looked good, when you felt spot-on, when people cheered, when you seemed wise, or when you got a promotion. When Jesus's love reigns through you, you win. Establish this as your success metric.

The *starts*:

1. **Start thanking instead of constantly apologizing.** Instead of saying, "I'm sorry I'm a burden," say, "Thank you for understanding that I am going to take a little extra time on this."

2. **Start adopting a "stop at nothing" determination.** When God sets you out to see things through, don't stop until, with God, you do.

3. **Start saying "not now," "maybe later," and "I'll have to reconsider that at another time."** Just because people ask for something doesn't mean you have to do it right away. Just because people text or email doesn't mean you have to respond right away.

4. **Start noticing.** Notice what you aren't following through on, so you stop committing to those kinds of things.

5. **Start knowing what the past means.** The definition of *past*, according to dictionary.com, is "completed, finished, and no longer in existence." Let this definition become your definition too. Let the past be the past. And let your present be your present.

Point 5: Fail to Plan, Plan to Fail

What Does Your Heart Incline to Do?

DO YOU:	ARE YOU:
bring out people's gifts?	an "illuminator"?
bring peace wherever you go?	a "peacemaker"?
provide guidance to others?	a "counselor"?
offer your hands of service?	a "worker"?
light up a room with joy?	a "joy bearer"?
continually unveil God's faithfulness?	a "faith sharer"?
seek justice?	a "justice seeker"?
uplift others?	an "encourager"?
tell the truth?	a "truth teller"?
sympathize with others?	a "sympathizer"?
gather people?	a "connector"?

DO YOU:	ARE YOU:
have tremendous vision?	a "visionary"?
shine creatively?	a "creator"?
discern things immediately?	a "wisdom carrier"?
manage details with skill?	an "organizational administrator"?
build into others?	a "disciple maker"?
see opportunity?	an "opportunity pointer"?
give thanks in all things?	a "praise infector"?
release others from bondage?	a "freedom warrior"?
spread resources?	a "giver"?
give lessons?	a "teacher"?
[fill in your own blank]	[fill in your own blank]

What Do You Love to Do?

What do you love to do? What you love doing may be what people say you are good at. You could be very good at accounting and hate every moment of it. I am talking about: What makes you come alive when you do it?

What makes you full of joy and excited to be alive?

Let's journey into this a little bit more.

First, pray, "God, open the eyes of my heart. I want to get a taste of what I love and what I am created to do. Will You lead me in this? Will You help me see what I love doing?" Then fill in these blanks:

I love it when I:

_____

_____

_____

_____

I come alive when I see this happening:

_____

_____

_____

I have always dreamed of:

_____

_____

_____

And remember: there is no dream or vision too impossible for God. There is nothing you might need that God can't provide.

Planning Tips & Reminders

Reminder 1: Small starts count big. A bicycle needs to build momentum to get going. The more you walk on a path, the more entrenched it gets and the wider it becomes. The more you make a recipe, the more you perfect it.

Tip 1: Just take the first step toward change today. Do the second step tomorrow.

Tip 2: Ask people for help.

Reminder 2: To write something down is to ink a plan in your mind to see it through.

At day sixty-six (the amount of time it takes to form a new habit), you want to not only have tackled heaps of laundry, mounds of paperwork, or your long commute but you also want to have seen through what matters most: love.

Tip 1: Detail the new life that you want to see through. Be detailed. Think of what adds value to your life and what detracts from it. Make a plan to add what counts and delete what doesn't.

Tip 2: Put love first. Live a life that does God's work first.

With this goal in mind, I have developed a corresponding Battle Ready Daily Prayer Journal to help you live a life that matters. This planner will help you to:

- *Acknowledge* and keep your "high goal."
- *Ask*, "God, what can I do today that backs up this unique goal/gifting You've given me?"
- *Act* on what is important first.
- *Abandon* what is not.
- *Accelerate*: move ahead with new habits in place.
- *Accomplish* the must-dos in a day.
- *Actively* put love first.

To revamp your schedule with God is to change your life. Radically.

<<<TO LEARN MORE >>> about the Battle Ready Daily Prayer Journal, visit: www.iambattle ready.com.

Assign your life. Chart what matters most.

Friends? Family? Time with God? Exercise? Fun? Education? Relaxation? Work? Eating? Commuting? Prayer?

Most people have sixteen waking hours in one day. Assign what matters to you in the hourly slots. Get a picture of your day, as God would want it to be. Under each section write some detailed notes (example: I will connect with God by reading the Bible. I will meet with a friend for lunch).

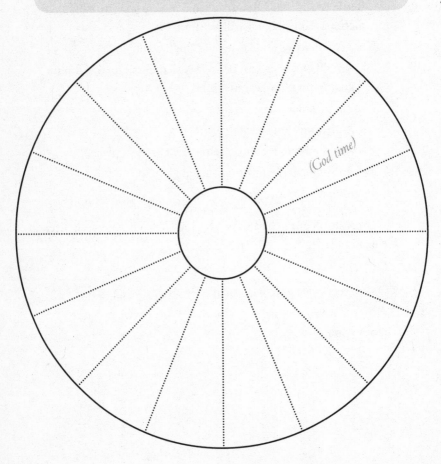

(God time)

Stop OVERSTUFFING

⚜

"COME *Follow* ME"

⚜

GO WITH *Faithfulness*

WHERE STRIVING CAN'T TAKE YOU

⚜

Ignore TAILGATERS

⚜

Schedule WHAT MATTERS MOST

A MIND TO CONQUER

A schedule is the DNA of life,
so if you don't like your life, change your schedule.

PRAY

Dear God, I don't want to focus so much on the mundane that I miss Your miraculous. I want You. I want You in all ways. You are the only One who will fulfill me. You are my best gift. Help me to know this and to rise up in what You are calling me to. I trust You. Increase my faith. In Jesus's name. Amen.

WRITE THREE THINGS YOU'RE THANKFUL FOR

1. _____

2. _____

3. _____

ENTER YOUR MIND

Need a great idea? Take a shower! Inspiration comes when we "feel great and relaxed." "Taking a warm shower, exercising, driving home," are all things that put us in chill mode. At times like these, our "chances of having great ideas . . . are a lot higher."[6] Give your mind space to think and the right answer might just pop into your mind.

And, yes, you do have enough space, time, and resources.

It's human nature to fill the time and space available to us. This phenomenon, known as Parkinson's Law, states that, 'Work expands so as to fill the time available for its completion.' Other variations of the principle include "*The more money you earn the more money you spend,*" or "*The bigger the available space, the more junk it can hold.*"[7]

EXAMINE YOUR STORY

1. What did you learn through this chapter?
2. What might God be calling you to, right now, to switch things up?
3. How has your busyness, overscheduled-ness, and overwhelmed nature negatively impacted those you love? Your relationship with God? Your heart?
4. What does it look like to lose your life for God's sake?

EXPLORE WITH GROUP STUDY

1. What did you learn from your personal study time?
2. What things do you intentionally or unintentionally mess up? Can you think of a story in which your busy nature caused catastrophe, an issue, or a heart problem to happen?
3. What in your life have you overstuffed? What pain is it causing you?
4. What do overstuffers miss? What are you missing out on?
5. What is underneath your desire to be busy, to overfill your house, and to live with so much going on? What fear exists? Are you trying to please others?
6. What doubts do you have about God if you don't do more? What truths does Scripture provide for each of these?
    For example:
    Will God show up?
    Will He really take care of me, in the space of my unknowing?
    Will I end up okay if I don't do all this stuff?

7. Of the ten things to stop doing ASAP, is there one that you can start today?
8. What calling most stood out to you? What do you think God might be leading you to? How are your wheels turning?

A CHRIST-CENTERED PRINCIPLE
GOD BLESSES

Simplicity that seeks God above all

But seek first the kingdom of God and his righteousness, and all these things will be added to you. (Matt. 6:33 ESV)

Warrior Mind-Set Nine

The One with Her Eye on the Prize
Goes Home with the Trophy

(Eternity)

Clarity about what matters provides clarity
about what does not.

Cal Newport, *Deep Work*

Point 1: What I Was Missing (and You Might Be Too)

I always wanted to do great things for God. At least, that's what I told Him. It was halfway true. The other half of me was deathly afraid of it.

But I still talked a lot about it. My life spoke too: nothing changed. I "did" church, watched TV, and did other normal stuff. I couldn't figure out why God didn't break through. Why didn't He do some wild miracle, like send me a burning bush or something?

Reflecting back, I can see: I aspired much but changed nothing.

I continued to go out and party.

I continued to want things for myself first.

I continued to make no time for God.

I continued to ache for men to love and desire me.

I continued to be obsessed with how I looked.

I demanded radical intervention but gave no room for breakthrough connection.

It's often far easier to pay God lip service and to halfway deny Him than it is to actually change.

Maybe you're there today. Maybe you love God but aren't sure you really would die for Him.

Point 2: Practical and Radical Heart Change Starts with This

I want my husband to know my heart completely, care for my vulnerabilities, and respond to my needs. He wants me to relate to his struggle, respect his character, and trust his ways. We're different.

Whenever we talk about this, my husband wisely summarizes our next step like this: "Kelly, we just need to get into each other's world."

He is right. When someone gets into my "world," I feel truly known.

For instance, when my husband says to me, "Kelly, I see all you're going through with the kids and your writing and your ministry. I know it is hard, but keep going; you are on the right path," I feel seen, loved, and cared for.

When my husband is in my world, it means the world to me.

God is always in our world. "The Holy Spirit . . . is in you. . . . You are not your own" (1 Cor. 6:19). The Spirit in us:

- Reveals Christ to us (John 15:26).
- Leads us in the right way (John 16:13).
- Helps us in our weakness (Rom. 8:26–27).
- Pleads for our needs (Rom. 8:26–27).

- Prepares us for ministry (Luke 4:18).
- Helps us remember we're God's daughters (Rom. 8:16).
- Brings freedom (2 Cor. 3:17).
- Comforts and encourages us (Acts 9:31).
- Empowers and strengthens us (Eph. 3:16).
- Fills our hearts with love (Rom. 5:5).
- Reveals God's truths (1 Cor. 2:10).
- Teaches us (John 14:26).

This is important, because when life breaks down to its highest degree, even the best of us can feel we are left in our house alone. Our body gets weak, our mental capacities stumble, our words fumble, and we feel isolated in our struggle. Yet even if everything feels lost, the Holy Spirit is not lost. He's in us. Pleading. Fighting on our behalf.

Years ago, when I delivered my daughter in under an hour, I had what was called an extreme labor. Because it was so fast, it caused debilitating pain. I thought I was going to die. I gripped the handle in the car so hard I fully expected to leave indents in it. In my moment of crisis, all I had was God. All I knew was, even though we were stuck in traffic, He heard me, He knew, and He understood. He could comfort me. His Spirit at work in my world was my only hope.

There, in the midst of my small glimpse of hell, God my only hope.

He understood.

God was the *only* answer. The one to whom I basically said, "God, I only want You. I'll do anything for You. I see You are all that matters."

What strikes me today is that we don't have to wait for the moment we're on death's doorstep to get serious about God. We don't have to wait for our own life-threatening moment to confess, "God, I'm all-in now and I will do anything, *no matter what*."

We can choose to be all-in today, no matter what, no matter the cost. This is our God-given moment. The time is *now*.

Point 3: The Most Important Thing We're Almost Always Forgetting

After going to the store, I stuff the fridge. I put the healthy stuff in the back, forget about it for a week and a half, and then pull out the box of salad—all moldy. Yuck.

In the same way, I often forget eternity is "back there."

I forget:

1. I'm dying.
2. Faith, hope, and love—Jesus is my forever-reality.
3. One day my show ends.

When we forget our show ends, life gets moldy. We settle into complacency. We think, *I'll do stuff for Jesus later. I'm all right. I'll fix things another time.*

Truth is, we don't know if we'll have later.

We are here one moment, gone the next.

At home with Chunky Monkey today, with Jesus tomorrow.

Temporal. Then with Jesus . . . forever.

Our moment is now. Kingdom come! This is our do-or-die moment. Do . . . or die to the feeling you could have done more but you wasted your life and now you hate yourself for it. Then die.

Do. Or. Die.

Do today what God is calling us to, so we don't die with

a lack of enthusiasm,

wasted days,

a boring existence,

a fear of other people,

a lack of fervor,

no vision or calling,

a "maybe later" mentality,

an uncommitted life,

guilt,

hoarding tendencies,

bitterness,

dissatisfaction,

hopelessness, or

a stupid settledness around earth's lesser things.

I like the phrase "Do or die." It reminds me of biker chicks. Women belonging to the same club, one with some cool emblem on the back of their leather jackets that conveys some message like, "Citizen of heaven" (Phil. 3:20), or "Our days on earth are like a shadow" (1 Chron. 29:15), or "To live is Christ, to die is gain" (Phil. 1:21).

These women seem like the type to seize that "do" so they don't die with the sense they just sat at home and called themselves a loser all the time. They'd get out there and take a risk. Look like a fool or whatever.

What if we did this?

What if we let all of God in now, rather than sitting around constantly dulled by entertainment and news? What if we stepped out rather than just biding our time? What if we believed more in the power of God to change lives rather than in our powerlessness to ever be more than we are?

The Lion is still roaring, and He wants us to roar out in the world with all we are, with all we have, reliant on Him. The time is now. You are breathing for a reason. If you are alive, God's plan for your life is in motion.

Help yourself gain your *go* by dwelling on verses like these:

I know all the things you do, and that you have a reputation for being alive—but you are dead. Wake up! Strengthen what little remains, for even what is left is almost dead. I find that your actions do not meet the requirements of my God. Go back to what you heard and believed at first; hold to it firmly. Repent and turn to me again. If you don't wake up, I will come to you suddenly, as unexpected as a thief. (Rev. 3:1–3 NLT)

So you also must be ready, because the Son of Man will come at an hour when you do not expect him. (Matt. 24:44)

And when the Chief Shepherd appears, you will receive the crown of glory that will never fade away. (1 Pet. 5:4)

"He will wipe every tear from their eyes. There will be no more death" or mourning or crying or pain, for the old order of things has passed away. (Rev. 21:4)

And if I go and prepare a place for you, I will come back and take you to be with me that you also may be where I am. (John 14:3)

And this is eternal life, that they know you, the only true God, and Jesus Christ whom you have sent. (John 17:3 ESV)

Look! I stand at the door and knock. If you hear my voice and open the door, I will come in, and we will share a meal together as friends. Those who are victorious will sit with me on my throne, just as I was victorious and sat with my Father on his throne. (Rev. 3:20–21 NLT)

Do-or-die gals live all-out today. They know God is not dead and neither are they. God is alive and well. Additionally, the Holy Spirit is in them, equipping them and pouring out from within them as they live on mission. These women are unstoppable.

Point 4: Five Renewing Thoughts

Do-or-die is difficult. I won't say it's easy. Embrace that it is hard. Really hard. For instance, just the other day, as I was reading the Bible, I felt conviction rise up within me.

God: *Kelly, your selfish ambition is straight-up demonic.*

Me: *What? Me?!*

God: "But if you have bitter jealousy and selfish ambition in your hearts, do not boast and be false to the truth. This is not the wisdom that comes down from above, but is earthly, unspiritual, *demonic*." (James 3:14–15 ESV, emphasis added)

Spirit-in-us, because He loves us, doesn't let us get away with stuff that wants to hurt us.

So while I wanted to pretend I didn't hear God, the new do-or-die biker girl in me had to admit the truth: I'd been so focused on myself, I'd recently missed being there for a friend in need.

I didn't *sow* time with her, nor *reap* peace, so I didn't *see* our relationship grow from this. Bad investment.

We all know bad investments, but do we know good ones? How to make kingdom deposits that don't end up feeling like emotional withdrawals?

We once again renew our thoughts. Here are five ways to renew your thoughts to help you live fully invested:

First thought: *I live to exemplify Christ.*

Therefore become imitators of God [copy Him and follow His example], as well-beloved children [imitate their father]; and walk *continually* in love [that is, value one another—practice empathy and compassion, unselfishly seeking the best for others], just as Christ also loved you and gave Himself up for us, an offering and sacrifice to God [slain for you, so that it became] a sweet fragrance. (Eph. 5:1–2 AMP)

Second thought: *Whatever I build on the foundation of love—Christ Jesus—lasts.*

But if anyone builds on the foundation with gold, silver, precious stones, wood, hay, straw, each one's work will be clearly shown [for what it is]; for the day [of judgment] will disclose it. (1 Cor. 3:12–13 AMP)

Third thought: *I can experience God's love in incredible ways.*

> When [Jesus] had finished washing their feet, he put on
> his clothes and returned to his place. "Do you under-
> stand [*ginōskō*] what I have done for you?" he asked them.
> (John 13:12)

Ginōskō means "get a knowledge of, experientially." Jesus
essentially asked them, "Did you feel? Deeply understand?
Do you truly realize and know in your heart what I just did
for you?"

God invites us to experience love. Why? So we may come

> to know [practically, through personal experience] *the love
> of Christ which far surpasses [mere] knowledge* [without
> experience], that you may be filled up [throughout your
> being] to all the fullness of God [so that you may have
> the richest experience of God's presence in your lives,
> completely filled and flooded with God Himself]. (Eph.
> 3:18–19 AMP, emphasis added)

Experience surpasses knowledge. Plus, as it pertains to
the science of our mind, experiences work to change our
thought life. They form new beliefs.

Fourth thought: *No matter how bad my story, there will come
His all-surpassing glory.*

> For our light and momentary troubles are achieving for us
> an eternal glory that far outweighs them all. (2 Cor. 4:17)

God's best is coming for you.

Fifth thought: *With perseverance, I can press on, even when I
am not perfect.*

> Therefore, since we are surrounded by such a great cloud
> of witnesses, let us throw off everything that hinders and

the sin that so easily entangles. And let us run with perseverance the race marked out for us. (Heb. 12:1)

Imperfectly but diligently, press on.

Point 5: Two "If" Statements to Remember

If we need a reminder that this is our one shot, we can:

- Drive by a cemetery.
- Read old eulogies online or look at the obituaries.
- Return to 1 Corinthians.
- Envision looking back on our life for what it was.
- Set a reminder on our phone, "Make it count!"
- Read stories online of old-age women who felt like they lived for "what mattered."
- Recommit our heart every morning to purity and focused living.
- Watch the movie *Beaches* 110 times.
- Look back at the end of each day and ask God, "Where did I serve You today?"
- Visit a hospice center.

If the going gets tough and we need more incentive, we can remember:

- God has a crown reserved for us; it is the ultimate prize. "Run in such a way as to get the prize . . . a crown that will last forever" (1 Cor. 9:24–25).
- God will reward and repay us for what we feel we've lost.
- God "will repay each person according to what they have done" (Rom. 2:6).
- We will "reap a harvest" if we "do not give up" (Gal. 6:9).

- God has incredible things prepared for us, as a result of our love (1 Cor. 2:9).

God, today, starting right now, in our lives, may: "your kingdom come, your will be done on earth as it is in heaven" (Matt. 6:10).

<<<GET A FREE >>> do-or-die biker chick computer screensaver image for a daily reminder that will keep you focused. Download it at www.iambattle ready.com.

THE *Holy Spirit*

IS IN YOUR WORLD

YOU'RE *Dying*

BE A "*Do or Die*"
BIKER CHICK

A MIND TO CONQUER

*Better is one moment on fire than a thousand lived
with the dull ache of a wasted life.*

PRAY

*Father, may I keep my eyes on You. This is my battle cry. This
is my heart. I want to keep You in the front of my mind, for
You are what stabilizes my mind. Pour grace out on me and
help me. I need You. I want Your kingdom to come on earth
as it is in heaven. Please show up, God, with the fullness of
Your power in my life. Amen.*

WRITE THREE THINGS YOU'RE THANKFUL FOR

1. _____

2. _____

3. _____

ENTER YOUR MIND

Love, kindness, and a giving spirit are good for us.

- Generosity in marriage leads to a happier marriage.[1]
- Those who serve are 76 percent healthier, 94 percent more likely to be in good spirits, and 78 percent less stressed.[2]
- More kindness equals less anxiety.[3]
- People feel "stronger," "calmer," "less depressed," and have "increased feelings of self-worth" as a result of acting kind to others.[4]

Think: Loving, giving, and caring lead to living well.

EXAMINE YOUR STORY

1. Does your life feel thrilling or complacent? Why? What do you think holds you back? Why?

2. Look back to the list of what the Spirit does when He enters your world. What feels most impactful to your heart? Write out new thoughts based on these truths. (Example: the Spirit of God frees me from my mind that condemns me.)

3. Encourage your heart. Based on this chapter, write out all the ways God wants to specifically enter your situation. Ask Him to speak into it. Write down His words to your heart.

4. What would it look like for you to really "do or die" with God? What would it look like for you to die to your ways and to live according to His?

5. Write your own selfish-to-selfless thoughts. Return to them as you confront difficult situations.

EXPLORE WITH GROUP STUDY

1. What did you learn from your personal study time?

2. Why do you forget life is short? How does this hold you back in life from the "best" things?

3. How might you choose to remember life is short?

4. What would it look like in your life to let the Spirit in you to work out from you? How might your daily moments be changed? What would you need to address?

5. What renewing thought most stood out to you? Why?

6. Talk about heaven. Discuss related Scripture. What will be best about heaven?

A CHRIST-CENTERED PRINCIPLE
GOD BLESSES

A "Thy Kingdom come, Thy will be done" perspective

Blessed is the man who makes the LORD his trust, who does not turn to the proud, to those who go astray after a lie! (Ps. 40:4 ESV)

Intermission Three

A Minding Grace Note

Dear Reader,

I want you to know: whether you implement every tip in this book or don't adopt a single one, as a child of God, you are still equally loved by Jesus. There is no amount of work that suddenly qualifies as "enough." There is no ladder you have to climb to finally find yourself in His grace. There is no threshold of merit you need to work up to. You are His. The words in this book are meant to be magnets that draw you to Him, that help you clear your mind, and that lead you to renewal. They aren't cure-all answers; Jesus is the only cure-all answer. His peace is left for you to take, so take it and rest in the truth that as you come weary, He'll leave you filled with rest. Jesus paid for your freedom. It's yours. This book just helps the truth of your belonging in Christ come to light. I hope.

Love,
Kelly

For it is by grace you have been saved, through faith—and this is not from yourselves, it is the gift of God—not by works, so that no one can boast. (Eph. 2:8–9)

Warrior Mind-Set Ten

Say "God Can, and I Will Rest in That"

(Positivity)

You are not a victim. You can control your reactions. You do have a choice.

Caroline Leaf, *Switch On Your Brain*

Point 1: One Way or the Other Thinking: Move Forward or Step Back

I can't write this chapter.

I keep on telling myself this. Especially after last night, a hellish, nightmarish, torturous night. *I feel horrible. Tired. Brain-dead. I can't.*

It's impossible.

Last night I ripped the covers off and pulled them back on nearly a hundred times. I flipped and flopped. I sweated up a storm. I woke for long periods of time. My mind was beaten.

So I can't. It won't happen.

I'm useless. I can't share deep and important things of God as it pertains to the mind. Can I?

I suppose at this point I have two choices:

A. Declare myself incapable, shut it all down, and not write.
B. Declare God capable, and write anyway.

Following through with Avenue A looks like me saying:

- I am too tired.
- My mind is broken.
- I have no good points.
- There is too much to weed through.
- I'm dumb now.
- I'll mess up.
- Everyone will hate it all.
- I don't feel like it.
- There are a hundred other things I need to do to accomplish this.
- I need more information.

It looks like me doing nothing.
Proceeding along Avenue B is to say:

- I am strong because my God is strong.
- I will find my way; God is faithful to unveil it.
- I am renewed in Christ Jesus; He can overcome a foggy mind.
- I am equipped to do this work because God has called me to it.
- I am able to stand on all the promises of God, no matter how I feel.
- I am a daughter whom a good Daddy takes care of.
- I am reliant, and God loves that.
- I am stronger tired with Jesus than I am alert on my own.

It looks like saying, "God has this, even if I feel I don't."

See the difference? Avenue A inhibits calling; Avenue B creates it.

Avenue A thinking says, "Quit." Then, tomorrow, it speaks even meaner, saying, "Way to go, Kelly. Now you have less time and you're behind. Now you're really stuck." Day by day, you less and less believe *you can* or *should*.

Discouragement breeds discouragement, failure breeds failure, and mean inner dialogues get meaner until you say, "No doubt, I am going to lose."

You throw in the towel. And you feel happy about it. Relieved, even.

Avenue A thinking tells a mind to step back.

Avenue B thinking, on the other hand, relies not on the human mind but on the mind of Christ. The natural mind (A) might fully see hardship, issues, and limitations, but the Spirit mind (B) shifts away from all that to see faith—God's coming victory. It speaks, "This is God's territory! Anything can happen here."

It talks like David, who said, "The Lord is the stronghold of my life—of whom shall I be afraid? . . . For in the day of trouble he will keep me safe in his dwelling; he will hide me in the shelter of his sacred tent and set me high upon a rock" (Ps. 27:1, 5).

It says, *God is coming through. Period.* It keeps going.

This mind dwells on the "more" God can do. In doing this, it builds positive momentum. Hope breeds more hope. Faith breeds more faith. And the mind harnesses the truth, "With God anything is possible."

Avenue B thinking propels a mind and life forward.

Do you see the difference? Avenue A is fleshly territory. Avenue B is Spirit victory.

In my case, B thinking sounds like this: *I can write, despite how I feel, because the God of all might fights for me. It is not my pretty words that will bring freedom but His Spirit at work.* With Avenue B thinking, the pressure is off!

Which avenue does your mind travel?

Consider this: when an issue emerges—a chronic infection, a stolen online identity, a family death, a too-high cost of living predicament, a child with a health issue, infertility, depression, a job from the depths of Hades, kids who are running amuck, a husband who is lost, people who are injurious, relationships that are absent or broken, doctor bills, a moral dilemma—what do you tend to think?

* I am ruined.
* I am a loser.
* I am dense.
* I am at a loss for words.
* No one sees me.
* I am taken advantage of.
* I am the only one God doesn't love.
* No one cares about me.
* This always happens.
* My life is out of control.
* People always hurt me.
* I am walking bad luck.
* I am ugly, worthless, or useless.
* I hate myself.
* I always cause more issues.
* People always hurt me.
* [Fill in the blank]

Do your thoughts sink you or remind you how Jesus carries you?

Do you step back, and think *I can't,* or think forward by ruminating on how *God will. God will be with me (Josh. 1:9). God will pull through for me. God will fight for me (Exod. 14:14). God will help me.*

God will.

So after you have suffered a little while, [God] *will* restore, support, and *strengthen you*, and he will place you on a firm foundation. (1 Pet. 5:10 NLT, emphasis added)

If God says He will, He will. "God is not human, that he should lie" (Num. 23:19). Why do we doubt Him?

We don't need to be perfect, brilliant, or overwhelmingly funded. God is all of those things. And more.

Do you believe this? How do you think? Do you say:

- I will never, ever . . .
- This always . . .
- I can't ever . . .
- I will always be . . .
- This will never change . . .
- It is impossible that . . .

These thoughts rip away a woman's crutches a second before God's miracle shows up. Christ is powerful. You meet His power when you meet His Word and get it all-up-and-into your life.

SOW GOD'S WORD > > >
REAP NEW THOUGHTS > > >
SEE NEW FAITH

How do we sow God's Word? We speak it aloud. The more we actively engage a thought, the more we remember *that* thought. This is why we recite a new person's name aloud if we want to recall it when they get back from the bathroom. This is why we read our high school social studies book aloud rather than internally

Pick which place you tend to speak from . . .

"The Desert of Not Enough"	**"Jesus Is More Than Enough"**
This desert is dry land. There is no time, water, resources, goods, hope, money. There is a lot of worry, striving, and control.	There is a table set here of great food. With far less fear, agony, and worry, this is a place of peace, glory, truth, life, hope, peace, trust, and rest.

running through it. The words we speak tend to settle into our brain.

> It is the same with my word.
>> I send it out, and it always produces fruit.
> It will accomplish all I want it to,
>> and it will prosper everywhere I send it. (Isa. 55:11 NLT)

We want to not only read God's Word but allow it to drive our fruit-producing life. We want the words to come off the pages so they settle into our hearts . . . then our thoughts . . . then our actions . . . then our future.

We don't speak aloud to establish a perfect American Dream life or to create 2 Porsches, a few Louis Vuitton handbags, and a show-off life; that is not at all what we are talking about here. We do it with a heart set on Jesus. We do it with a heart that pursues His heart, His goals, and His ways.

How did Jesus speak? We never heard Him say, "I can't ever, this always hangs me up, I've never been able to . . ." Jesus spoke the language of miracles, potential, vision, healing, renewal, and hope. He saw what others couldn't. He believed in the incredible. His words were actively prayerful. And He never made back-alley agreements with the devil about things He couldn't, wouldn't, or shouldn't do. He didn't lower himself down to earthly expectations or limitations.

Why do we?

What limiting, confining, or debilitating agreements have you made?

Change your script. Think forward, not backward.

Speak: "Jesus is life. He is redeeming life. He has great plans for my life. He is teaching me. His Spirit is freedom. What looks impossible, [insert that very thing here], I believe He will ultimately work for good. His will is a good will."

To think forward is to agree with what God has already said:

"All things are possible with God" (Mark 10:27).

"[I] will see the glory of God" (John 11:40).

God is equipping me for great works (John 14:12–14).

God lives in me, and I live in God (1 John 4:15).

My victory is "through our Lord Jesus Christ" (1 Cor. 15:57).

All authority in heaven and earth belongs to Jesus, and He is in charge of me (Matt. 28:18).

God will supply all my needs according to the riches of His glory in Christ Jesus (Phil. 4:19).

In every respect, my aim is to grow to be like Jesus (Eph. 4:15).

Speak up for Jesus. Let your voice proclaim the glory of the Lord so it is established within your belief system.

And don't be silenced. Even if the enemy has tried for decades to silence your words, don't be surprised. Of course he has! Your voice so loudly matters. Science proves our words give direction to our mind. We not only speak a truth to learn a truth but as we speak it our mind comes to believe it. What is repeated, becomes real. It's no wonder Scripture tells us, "Bless the LORD, O my soul" (Ps. 104:1 KJV), to establish His Word in our hearts (Job 22:22), and that "the soothing tongue is a tree of life" (Prov. 15:4). Promises that ring loud as truth dispel doubt. Speaking trains us in believing.

Just consider how we started faith . . .

1. We declared, or spoke.
   "If you *declare* with your mouth, 'Jesus is Lord . . .'"
2. We believed.
   ". . . and believe in your heart that God raised him from the dead, you will be saved" (Rom. 10:9, emphasis added).

Couldn't God have said, "If you feel, understand, or have knowledge in your heart Jesus is Lord"? Why the first part, "declare with your mouth"? I believe speaking belief in Christ solidifies truth in us. It says to our mind:

> You are now going Jesus's way.
>
> You belong to Jesus.
>
> You really do believe.
>
> You are proclaiming your God to all.
>
> Jesus is your Lord.
>
> Jesus is your keeper.
>
> You are sold out now!

His Word sustains all life.

> The Son is the radiance of God's glory and the exact representation of his being, sustaining all things *by his powerful word*. (Heb. 1:3, emphasis added)

As we speak as He speaks—His Word—in our mind and aloud . . . in practice and in deed . . . at night and in the morning . . . entering trials or emerging from them . . . our mind gains an awareness of God's power, breathing and living in our lives. *Whoa!* But if we don't, our mind becomes sustained by our thoughts . . . our effort, our distress, our whimsies, our demands, our impromptu reactions, our feelings, and our impulsive inclinations. *Yuck.*

Either way: reap, sow, see. Think and see it play out.

If we think we look like a hot mess in the morning, we'll feel like a hot mess through the day. Studies show our choice of clothing "primes the brain to function differently." This is astounding: thoughts focused on something as simple as what we wear have the power to dictate our identity.[1] No wonder we're told, "Put on Christ, like putting on new clothes" (Gal. 3:27 NLT). His identity recycled, day after day, is our only identity.

> Christ is in me, the hope of glory. (Col. 1:27)

Greater is He, in me, than he who is in the world. (1 John 4:4)

I am a chosen person. (1 Pet. 2:9)

I am God's special possession. (1 Pet. 2:9)

By His stripes, I am healed. (Isa. 53:5)

Faith is not us; it is Jesus. Jesus bulldozes man-made obstacles out of the way so we can move forward.

Point 2: Ten Reasons Forward Thinking Is Mind-Altering

A month ago, we buckled the kiddos into the car and headed down the highway for a day of fun. Unexpectedly, I was jolted. My husband had swerved left. He said, "Ugh . . . I had no room on the right. I had to swerve."

Thing was, as I saw it, he had plenty of room. He had the same exact amount of room as before. All that changed was a construction wall placed a little outside of his lane.

His mind tricked him. Believing he didn't have enough space, he freaked.

Often, our mind tricks us the same way. We freak.

We freak when we don't believe we have enough:

Resources: people, help, ideas, materials, or information to get the job done.

Ability: smarts, beauty, know-how, wisdom, grace, education, life experience, track record, physical strength, or knowledge to get ahead.

Time: space to succeed, years left, room to improve, spaces to meet with God, or span to make a difference.

Market share: personal branding, an edge up on other women, material items, wealth, goods, appearances, presence, or charisma to be seen.

Where do you feel you don't have enough? Circle the above areas.

Let's think back for a moment to my son at that big buffet spread. Remember: when he felt limited, he was restrictive. But when he saw the unlimited nature of what was before him, he felt unlimited in giving and loving.

Likewise, when we don't think we have enough, we usually jerk away and grip life tightly. We disaster-plan. We build a bunker. Hide out. Bury our talents.

This is not what we want. We don't want to swerve and divert God's best things.

My husband's lane was never smaller. His vision of it was. This often holds true for us too. Yet the storehouses of God's goodness, provision, and care are open. Yet the riches of His glorious inheritance still belong to us. Yet the peace of Christ still awaits.

Will we choose to focus on Christ's immensity or our scarcity?

Our lack? Bare accounts? Dry lands? Hopeless situations? Horrible grieving? No answers? No hope? What we don't have? Where we've been ripped off? Where we're going down? What people have done? Why we can't ever be the same? How God injured us?

Or abundant life?

Just because we see thirty thousand reasons we're bound to fail doesn't mean there aren't a million reasons why, because of Christ, we've won.

In elementary school, there were a million reasons why I was bound to fail. I wrote my letters backward. I couldn't differentiate the word C-A-T from D-O-G. I got tested for all kinds of learning disabilities. I stayed back in third grade. I had every reason, from my point of view, to say, "I'll never be smart. I'll always be dumb. I can't write worth a lick. People think I am the worst. I'll always be criticized."

I had every reason *not* to write this book. I had every reason to feel unqualified.

Yet, while I saw the million reasons why I was bound to fail, I believe God saw infinite reasons why He can do anything.

I find it a miracle I'm an author. If He did it with me, He can do anything with anyone. There's a good chance God laughs at all we think impossible.

The point is, we have enough because we have God. We have victory because Jesus now reigns in victory. His victory is our personal victory. Forward thinkers often return back to this point.

They understand *forward thinking*, done again and again, is life-giving. Here are ten reasons why:

1. It teaches your mind to grow.

     Like elastic, a mind stretches in the direction it's pulled. The more we pull it toward God, the more it loosens and lets in His peace, joy, and hope.
2. It makes your battleground a mind-renewing ground.

     A hard time is a prime time to change a mind, because a mind remembers "strong" or "weighty" times with more accuracy.[2]
3. It helps you see your mighty God as mighty.

     Hardly ever do we focus on the first two days Jesus stayed in the grave. What we focus on is the third day. The day of breakthrough. Forward thinking renews hope in God's bust-out abilities.
4. It establishes barriers.

     Doubters breed doubt. Gossipers breed gossip. Criticizers breed criticism. Forward thinking forces us to consider what voices we let into our mind, what friendships we keep, and what life we're after.
5. It gets us to the heart of the matter.

     If you speak something and you don't believe it, your heart will inform you quickly. Recognize unbelief and bring it to God.
6. We learn staying ability beats raw ability.

We learn to lean on Daddy's gifts versus our IQ, to rely on His providence versus our preparedness and His equipping power versus our declarations we are powerless. No matter how good we feel, we learn it is His grace that carries us through.

7. We comprehend that change doesn't happen independently of God.

    Forward thinking helps us to pray for greater belief.

8. It gets our mind off "them" and onto "us."

    We realize God can radically change our life without even laying a finger on their life. We are freed from being beholden to people.

9. We can let go of our strong responses and find love:

    • if someone is judging us. That is their mind issue.

    • if someone is comparing themself to us. That is their insecurity.

    • if someone is criticizing us. That is their junk to work through.

    Your sole goal, though, is always *to love*. Certainly, examine your heart, but if you find no issue, move on.

10. We start to pour out Jesus Christ wherever we go.

    Just as kids pick up their parents' worst habits, we can pick up Christ's best.

Point 3: The Five-Point Mind-Renew

When my son was itty-bitty, he was cute, but he wasn't very bold. At the park, he was hesitant. He'd look down at his feet and wonder if he really could jump. He'd freeze on the monkey bars. We couldn't get him to move. Ugh. My husband and I so badly wanted him to believe in himself. But despite our cajoling, he was a rock. Immovable.

Something had to change. So rather than pleading, "Come on, come on," or "You can, you can," we just began to speak up in his life. "Michael, you are courageous." We said it whenever the opportunity presented itself. We said it in the little and the big.

From that day forward, for the most part, we didn't stop. After a few weeks, something sparked in him. A "go" emerged. He started to believe the words were true. The more we said them, the more he believed. Until itty-bitty was brave.

What we speak over ourselves becomes our truth.

We tell our mind what to think. We can think:

I am always having a hard time.

I am in for it.

I am never going to see my life change.

I am far from doing things differently.

I am doubtful I can conquer my mind.

I am unsure.

I am cranky.

I am having a bad day.

I am never going to amount to anything.

I am always hurting myself.

I am always finding myself in bad relationships.

Or we can speak like God speaks, using His Word. We can say (try also inserting your name in each line):

I can do exceedingly abundantly more than I can ask or imagine in Christ Jesus (Eph. 3:20).

I am enduring in trials and will discover an eternal weight of glory one day (2 Cor. 4:17).

I am in Christ, and no one can stand against Him (Rom. 8:31).

I am provided for by the ultimate Provider (2 Pet. 1:3).

I am not taken down by weapons; no weapon formed against me shall prosper (Isa. 54:17).

I am being made into the image of Christ Jesus (2 Cor. 3:18).

I am growing; my mind is being transformed to understand God's will (Rom. 12:2).

I am forgiven, pure, and holy because of Jesus (Eph. 1:4).

I am loved, and He who died for love will eternally keep me (Jude 24).

I am marked with the seal of the Holy Spirit; I belong to God (Eph. 1:13).

I am represented by *the King of Kings. People are not the predictors of my destiny* (1 Tim. 6:15; Gal. 6:5).

I am fully loved by Christ (John 3:16).

I am forgiven immediately when I confess a mistake and am in God's good graces (1 John 1:9).

I am chosen to do good works in Christ Jesus. They have been prepared for me and I will walk in them (Eph. 2:10).

I am open to receiving the "incomparable riches of his grace" (Eph. 2:7).

I am blessed with good gifts from a good Father (Ps. 85:12).

I am strong in God, even when I feel weak (2 Cor. 12:9).

I am covered under God's feathers (Ps. 91:4).

I am equipped with God's shield of protection (Ps. 91:4).

I am under the cover of the dwelling of the Most High God (Ps. 91:9).

God will rescue me; I love Him and He loves me (Ps. 91:14).

When I call on God, He will answer me (Ps. 91:15).

God will be with me in my time of trouble; He will deliver me (Ps. 91:15).

Add yours here: _____

God's Word reshapes us internally so the external becomes inconsequential. This is the power of God activated.

It doesn't matter how smart or dumb, how big or small, how strong or weak you are—God doesn't discriminate with His grace.

For example, my son, the itty-bitty one grown five-years big, was practicing running not long ago. He gave his all. He pushed. Afterward, he was tired and sweaty. I was curious. I wanted to know how "forward thinking" would work within him. I told him, "Son, do it again. This time, go into your super-speed gear. I believe God in you and with you will help you. Ask Him for help."

He looked at me inquisitively. But then he believed; he trusted God to help him. He set up on the starting line. I screamed, "Go!" and he shaved a few seconds off his time.

Interesting.

His belief helped him to do something he never would have done without faith. Now, here, I can't delineate where our God-given effort and God's miraculous working come together. This is beyond me. All I know is when they both move, they hold hands well together.

What I also know is that we may feel very called by God to be an ultra-marathoner or to scale Mount Everest. So we may do it and give it our all, through faith, and yet not see anything come of it. Does this mean we failed? I don't believe so. It is impossible to please God without faith. He rewards those who diligently seek Him (Heb. 11:6). His working goes far beyond our seeing. And by hope, founded on faith, we gain strength.

"Those who hope in the LORD will renew their strength" (Isa. 40:31).

There is always more than meets the eye. Choose to believe. Start by saying, "With Christ, all things are possible." Then prepare yourself for the battle of standing strong in faith, using this five-point mind-renew:

1. **Tell yourself, "I'm entering a battle."**

    If you know you're entering a battle, you'll get ready to fight. This is good. Life is a battle full of trials, difficulties, and combat. Acknowledging this tells your mind, *I am fighting to win.* It also indicates, *It will be hard, there will be times I fall, but I'll get back up again.* It helps set up a will of perseverance and endurance. It keeps in mind the prize at the end of the days.

    Gain a Mind to Take Action

    - If you hear, "Are you sure you should do this?" "Who are you to . . .?" or "I heard about another person going through that and they [insert horrible issue here] . . ." let these words slide right off your shoulders.

    - Think of the forces of God behind you as you love. If God is for you, who can be against you (Rom. 8:31)? Have faith and do His will. God is the God of the angel armies!

    - Abandon scrutinizing and down-talking your every tactic. Warriors see the calling, then move swiftly. Don't give too much room to ruminating; you'll lose your sprint. Run with God into the battle. There's no bullet He can't sway.

2. **Consider what God might be up to.**

    We may do something without a purpose, but I don't believe God ever does.

    Gain a Mind to Take Action

    - Ask yourself: "How might God be using this hardship for my benefit? To change something? To make Himself known? What might God be up to?"

    - Ponder: What, by faith, might God be doing?

    > Finally, brothers and sisters, whatever is true, whatever is noble, whatever is right, whatever is pure, whatever is lovely, whatever is admirable—if anything is excellent or praiseworthy—think about such things. (Phil. 4:8)

- Think of fun times. Dwell on memories of fun, laughter, and joy, rather than your pain, agony, guilt, remorse, anger, abuse, distrust, frustration, or irritation.
- Live one day at a time. If you aren't living in tomorrow, why should your mind dwell there? God works in the here and now.
- Add the word *but* to your negative thinking. Example: "I am not able to lose this weight, *but* with God I can do it. All things are possible with Him, and He'll help me see it through."

3. **Exchange limitations for expectation.**

"Surely there is a future, and your hope will not be cut off" (Prov. 23:18 ESV).

Gain a Mind to Take Action

- Find the hope.

For example, rather than thinking, *It is a bad day*, think, *God is teaching me things today.*

Rather than thinking, *I'll never get out of debt*, think, *God is my provider. I am excited to see how He will show up.*

Rather than thinking, *That lady is a rude person who is mean*, think, *I don't know what she is going through in her life. I will ask God to help me love her.*

- Avoid assumptions. They are diversions leading you away from connection with God. They almost always kill love.

4. **Get in your secret garden.**

The secret garden is *prayer*. It's your escape. It's your place of planting new seeds. It's where God waters. It's where battles are won or lost. It's where a harvest is reaped.

Gain a Mind to Take Action

When you're praying, if your mind wanders to everything you need to do, keep a pad of paper next to you. Write things as they come up, then immediately return to where you were. But don't get your phone, scroll Facebook, or start texting. Keep your garden time just for you.

- Pray Scripture (as Paul prayed and as the Psalms go) over your life, out loud.

5. **Remind yourself.**

There are new mercies every day. And you are a new creation.

Gain a Mind to Take Action

Set up reminders affirming this truth on:

> a note on your mirror

> a pen-inked message on your hand

> a notecard in your wallet

> a pop-up reminder on your phone

> a screensaver on your computer

> notecards around your house

<<<PRINT >>> a Paper Positivity Bracelet. Wear it to remind you, minute by minute, to stay positive. Find it at www.iambattleready.com.

EITHER STEP BACK

OR *Think Forward*

YOUR BATTLEGROUND =

A *Mind-Renewing* GROUND

WHAT YOU *Speak*

OVER SELF BECOMES TRUTH

Consider WHAT GOD'S UP TO

A MIND TO CONQUER

If you decide you've already lost the war,
you've lost before you even begin.

PRAY

Father God, You are good. Help me to believe it. Help me to
rely on that fact. I need not fear You will kind-of-bless me
or sort-of-help me. You are 100 percent behind me, with me,
and for me. I am not left unchosen, unloved, or unwanted.
Thank You that, in all ways, You have my best interests in
mind. Help me believe. In Jesus's name. Amen.

WRITE THREE THINGS YOU'RE THANKFUL FOR

1. _____

2. _____

3. _____

ENTER YOUR MIND

Your brain has a "negativity bias." Rick Hanson, author of *Hard-wiring Happiness*, explains it like this:

> The brain evolved a built-in negativity bias. While this bias emerged
> in harsh settings very different from our own, it continues to oper-
> ate inside us today as we drive in traffic, head into a meeting, settle
> a sibling squabble, try to diet, watch the news, juggle housework,
> pay bills, or go on a date. Your brain has a hair-trigger readiness
> to go negative to help you survive.[3]

Try fighting it by:

1. Flooding your mind with what's redeemable.
2. Thinking of everything you're thankful for.
3. Remembering we all worry about far more than ever happens.
4. Being grateful for who God is.
5. Acknowledging the fact that you have a Savior who saves, a Provider who provides, and a Love who never fails.
6. Bouncing off of it by immediately focusing on something else.

EXAMINE YOUR STORY

1. What horrible things have you declared over your life? (Write the exact phrases.) What mean things have you thought about yourself? Others?
2. What kind of Avenue B thinking do you embrace? Avenue A?
3. How has Avenue A thinking held you back in life?
4. How can you begin to resuscitate yourself with the fact that God always shows up (Josh. 1:9), pulls through (Deut. 31:6), fights (Exod. 14:14), endures (Ps. 136), and gives power to those in need?
5. Are you known for using any of these phrases? Circle the ones you speak.
   - I will never, ever . . .
   - This always . . .
   - I can't ever . . .
   - I will always be . . .
   - This will never change . . .
   - It is impossible that . . .

EXPLORE WITH GROUP STUDY

1. What did you learn from your personal study time?

2. How can you help yourself quickly catch what is not profitable in your mind?

3. What would all-out, full belief in God look like in your life? What would you need to let go of? Embrace?

4. Share a struggle you're having a hard time with. Flood each person involved with God's truths as it relates to this. Write them down and hold on to them afterward.

5. Are limitations true or false? How so?

6. How have you seen God break the barriers in your life and in the lives of others? Share faith-building stories.

7. How can you, as a group, support each other in forward thinking? Be accountable to one another?

8. Consider a battle one of you might be going through. Put it through the five-point mind-renew process. See what you can come up with as it pertains to that issue. (And yes, when it comes to #4, pray over it!)

A CHRIST-CENTERED PRINCIPLE
GOD BLESSES

Jesus-centered positivity

I can do all this through him who gives me strength. (Phil. 4:13)

Warrior Mind-Set Eleven

She Who Realizes She Has Nothing to Lose Understands She Has Everything to Gain

(Intensity)

So, because you are lukewarm—neither hot nor cold—I am about to spit you out of my mouth.

Revelation 3:16

Point 1: What Matters Is What's in Your Hand

Imagine you are playing poker. No doubt, you're going to win; you just know it! You have four of a kind. It's a fantastic hand. It beats almost every other hand in poker.

But your best friend—and her attitude—makes you question things. She's shifting her shoulders with confidence. She gives you *the eye* and smiles *that* smile. And now you're not so sure. Your thoughts shift. *I'm going to lose. I'm going down. Her face says it all. How could I have ever thought I was going to win?*

You fold.

She flips.

Nothing. You gave up everything when she held nothing.

You lost because you doubted. Even though all along you held the winning hand. But you didn't believe. Belief was what mattered.

When we don't believe the hand of Jesus Christ has won, we fold in doubt. Then hate ourselves for it.

We fall like paupers when we had royal backing to fight like princesses. The enemy snarls an untouchable snarl and we run away, tail between our legs. We lose because we figure we're bound to.

Meanwhile, at our disposal is the fullness of God's resources. At our call is His strengthening ability. In Him we are conquerors, overcomers, and victors. We are daughters, united with Christ.

> For he raised us from the dead along with Christ and seated us with him in the heavenly realms because we are united with Christ Jesus. (Eph. 2:6 NLT)

But we get caught up in immediate issues—bills, turmoil, roughness, pain, and annoyances. We are apt to live like slaves to our burdens.

Do you live by the "spirit of sonship" or like a slave to circumstances?

It is easy to feel we're a slave to our circumstances. You wouldn't believe all that's transpired as I've written this book. The father of lies (John 8:44) is the ultimate poker player with the ultimate antagonizing face. He hisses in our ear, makes us forget what we do, and gives us the horrifying sense that our destruction is right around the corner. He knows children, faithless, feel defenseless. He barks loud, but this doesn't mean we have to fold.

We can choose to listen for his voice of intimidation, manipulation, and confusion. We can do this by acquainting ourselves with the somewhat predictable five-pronged attack that seeks to take us down. It sounds like this:

1. I'll make them doubt God is good.

   He knows: if we think God will hurt us, we'll run from Him.

2. I'll make them severely question their abilities.

He knows: if we focus on our insecurities, we won't rely on God's providing abilities.

3. I'll make them tally potential losses.

He knows: if we're deathly afraid of losing, we'll run, tail between our legs, away from our destiny.

4. I'll make them focus on their record, past, or naysayers' comments.

He knows: if we rehash the past, we'll relive it in the future.

5. I'll make them hate others.

He knows: filled with bitterness, we'll have little room left to be filled with God.

The stealer, killer, and destroyer of faith wants us to think:

God is distant.
He doesn't really love us.
He hardly ever helps us.

He wants to steal our good hand. If he accomplishes that, he makes us believe we lack destiny and we forgo our intensity. We fold. Discouraged, we then hide out and burrow deep down under our covers. We miss God's good works prepared for us in advance. *Poof.*

Point 2: Seven Vulnerabilities the Enemy Consistently Attacks (F.I.G.H.T.E.R.)

How do we expect to fight when many of us walk with our eyes on our smartphone, down a dark alley, wearing headphones? Head in the clouds, we walk like prime meat. Like little Red Riding Hoods waiting to be snatched. We're oblivious. Wake up!

We need to be alert by doing these three things:

1. Be Aware

"Be alert and of sober mind. Your enemy the devil prowls around like a roaring lion looking for someone to devour" (1 Pet. 5:8).

Fighter women are aware. Are you?

Charles Stanley came up with a useful acronym of times women should be aware of the enemy.[1] Building off of his, I created my own. Take note: F.I.G.H.T.E.R. women are most prone to enemy attack when they are:

Famished: "Can't think? Perfect," says the enemy.

Irritable: "Cranky? I can use you all the more to offend people and feel bad about yourself."

Gullible: "I'll tell you a lie and lead you astray in a split second."

Hurried: "Distracted with a hundred things, her devotion and adoration will go out the window."

Tired: "She'll feel so worn, she'll say, 'Why bother?'"

Extremely Emotional: "I'll get her so worked into a tizzy, she'll solely focus on how she feels and not on Jesus."

Removed: "Isolated Christians tend to feel unloved and unwanted and just where I want them."

Be a F.I.G.H.T.E.R. with an intensity about you. Fighters see what's coming on the horizon and proactively get in front of it. They don't pretend things will somehow work out okay and ignore the issues. They don't just wait around for the change they fear will hit. They don't worry endlessly about what could happen. They practically fortify their mind by seeing through the basics.

This looks like getting good sleep. Doing your physical workout. Getting together with friends. Spending time with God. Eating when you're hungry. Stopping when you're full. Putting Jesus first. Checking your emotions. Decluttering your schedule. Ditching distractions. Thinking forward. Sowing well. Or speaking the truth with love.

Do what you forget to do, so your mind doesn't forget truth. Then . . .

2. Prepare

When you make a cake, before you combine the wet and dry ingredients, you sift the flour. Why? You remove the unsavory clumps you don't want to end up eating. You also do this to produce a soft pile of powder-fine flour. Something that resembles purity.

Sifting is essential within a mind. To sift is to quickly identify the clumpy thoughts that do not belong—the sophisticated, proud, exalted, self-seeking, devious, manipulative, or anti-God thoughts. It is to then break them apart in order to mold them into truth. This is what it means to take "captive every thought to make it obedient to Christ" (2 Cor. 10:5). What remains is purity.

Like a clean table, this creates a great working place for God to shape a new thing. Here we tend to see transformation, which happens "with ever-increasing glory, which comes from the Lord, who is the Spirit" (2 Cor. 3:18).

When you kick the bad stuff out, you make room for the good to come in.

3. Be Full of Prayer

F.I.G.H.T.E.R. women pray like this:

A Prayer of Resolve That Repels Evil
   God, I believe! I believe You can do all things. I believe You can make a path for me where there is none. I believe You can forge wisdom where my mind is blank. I believe You can grant me greater faith. I believe You see me as a noble warrior. I believe even if everyone thinks poorly of me, leaves me, or forsakes me, You'll take care of me as my heart stays devoted to You in love. I believe You see my heart, delight in my loyalty, take note of my commitment, and notice my pursuit of You.

247

I am in Your good graces because of Jesus. No good thing do You withhold from me. You open the storehouses of Your love, grace, and providence and pour them down on me. Not because I've earned it but because You simply love me. I can rest in You. I am fully holy, fully righteous, and fully pure thanks to the spotless Lamb. I am a new creation in You. I accept Your love.

I submit to Your plan. Take me where You will; I am ready to go. Push me; I'll give way. Lead me; I am listening. Instruct me; You are life, peace, joy, and the only way. You are my victory, even if it looks different than I expect. I attest, if You are for me, who can be against me? If You are with me, nothing else matters. And if You're not in it, I don't know why I would want it to begin with. All I want is You. In Jesus's name I pray. Amen.

Sometimes gunshots can equal safety. Sound crazy?

Let me explain. One day I threw my arms up, pushed the screen door open, and headed out onto my suburban sidewalk. I couldn't jet off to Hawaii, but I could go on a walk. That's how I figured it anyway as I set off with God to escape the mountain-high stacks of dishes and the annoying sense I wasn't really that great of a mother. God, I knew, wanted time with me.

Feeling quite proud of myself for obeying and for abandoning all that I felt was attacking me, I headed toward a busy road. As I approached it, I kept considering God's faithfulness and how He protects me. Yet no sooner was I a few steps onto this busy road when gunshots sounded. Loud. Close. Deafening.

Would they hit me? Would this be it? Would my kids miss me?

Fear climbed all over me. I didn't know what to do. So I broke out in an all-out sprint home. I ran, heart thumping, wondering if a bullet would come my way.

I set out with God but ran home with fear.

Looking back, I don't know why I was so afraid. I am more safe in God's plan than anywhere else.

Whether I am in a drive-by shooting or in the heart of a hurricane or in the confines of a flu-laden emergency room, if God is there and He has called me there, I am safely within His plan. Far safer than where He doesn't want me to be.

It's an interesting thought, right?

The safest woman is not the one safeguarding her assets, her children, her house, or her well-being; she's the one abiding under the safety of God's love that moves her out to risky places.

This woman is untouchable, really. It doesn't matter where God brings her. Even if it's a terrorist-laden nation or a poverty-stricken community or a lions' den, the power of God welling up in her is her armor. It energizes and compels her. It renews her and establishes her faith.

We often think we are protected within our man-made walls of safety, but it really is by annihilating these figurative walls that we find the true protection we always wanted—because we find God. We find His protection too.

This is freeing. We can hold the hands of drug addicts, lie down next to a homeless person, talk to a prostitute, reach out to *that* spouse, kneel down and wash the feet of the girl we've hated for a long, long time . . . and it's in these moments we've never felt more alive.

The most powerful type of woman in the world is the one simply operating exactly where God wants her. Everything in her life is an adventure. It doesn't matter where she is—she could be at her kitchen counter, or doing the laundry, or kneeling.

God doesn't judge like we do. Everything with God is adventure if we let it be. Everything. And where He is, there is safety.

Locations don't matter. These are only earthly coordinates.

God can just as easily prompt you, as you fold laundry, to reach out to that one girlfriend who was about to start drinking again as He could have you adopt an orphan in Africa as you go on a mission trip. Neither is better than the other. Don't disqualify your place in the world. He could just as easily have you give a suicidal coworker a word of encouragement that changes it all as He could have you lead a million people to Jesus. Bathroom or prison, ballroom or basement, baby's room or bunker, God prompts us all to risky callings in all locations. Let go of the inadequacy you feel because of your coordinates or the appearance of your atmosphere.

Never confuse yourself: granite counters, daily lattes, big bank accounts, and manicured lawns don't equal safety. A husband can cheat on you there, or you can cheat on him with the pool guy. You can go get that pack of cigarettes or you can waste thousands on bathing suits. You can find depression or you can well up in so much critical anger that you convince yourself you're as bad as a far-off terrorist. Appearances confuse us.

Do they confuse you? Take a moment to consider . . .

- ☐ Are you sometimes afraid to fully let go and love God? Why?
- ☐ Do you feel full abandon might mean drastic life change and sacrifice?
- ☐ Are you worried God might call you to give up the things you most love?
- ☐ Do you have an underlying hesitancy you might be rejected by people if you were "all in"?
- ☐ Do you tend to feel safety is your highest pursuit?
- ☐ Do you think God might reject you, or notice your flaws then no longer want you?
- ☐ Do you feel that the bullets of life, the distractions that hit you, make it impossible to live sold-out?
- ☐ Are you too busy to live a life of complete abandon?

The fact of the matter is, we often:

- ☐ Hold ourselves back.
- ☐ Blame the world (issues, people, resources, barriers) for holding us back.
- ☐ Allow the enemy to hold us back.

Problems arise when we mentally, spiritually, physically, or emotionally stay where we were never meant to remain. Then, we feel suffocated, bitter, and held back. Don't permit safety to be a setback or a pullback to blah-ness.

Point 3: The 3L Battle Plan

If Jesus did not shirk back from the intensity of missional risk, why should we?

> Therefore be imitators of God, as beloved children. (Eph. 5:1 ESV)

If we are to imitate Christ, we must copy Him. To do this, let's embrace the 3L Battle Plan. We can emulate the Lion, Lamb, and Love.

First L: Jesus Is the Lion of Judah

> And I saw a mighty angel proclaiming in a loud voice, "Who is worthy to break the seals and open the scroll?" But no one in heaven or on earth or under the earth could open the scroll or even look inside it. I wept and wept because no one was found who was worthy to open the scroll or look inside. Then one of the elders said to me, "Do not weep! See, *the Lion of the tribe of Judah*, the Root of David, has triumphed. He is able to open the scroll and its seven seals." (Rev. 5:2–5, emphasis added)

As John's prophetic vision portrays, Jesus is the Lion of the tribe of Judah. As Lion, Jesus is able, worthy, and triumphant. Only He can open the scrolls. Only He rules. Victorious.

Jesus is the Victory, who is our victory.
If Jesus is Lion, how can we be lionlike too? We can:

- *Walk with the bold authority of Jesus Christ* (see Matt. 28:18; Luke 10:19). This means we know no person is too hardened for God's power to change them, no problem is too solidified to be softened by God's love, and no condition is too immovable for Jesus to kick it miles out of the way.

- *Put the enemy in his place.* You wouldn't go out of your way looking to kill a house ant, but you might a tarantula loose in your house. The point is, the enemy wants to kill threats. Be encouraged; opposition is often confirmation you're on the right path.

- *Refrain from giving the enemy ruling power he doesn't have.* "You, dear children, are from God and have overcome them, because the one who is in you is greater than the one who is in the world" (1 John 4:4).

- *Bind the enemy away.* We can say, "Through Jesus, His blood and sacrifice, I disarm the enemy. I stand in Jesus's strength and sacrifice. Right now, anything coming against me has no power. I am covered in Christ's blood and forgiven. And by His sacrifice I break the power of this lie: [insert here]. God says [insert here]." When you continually do this, the enemy eventually decides to go bark up another tree.

- *Decide continuous praising is our best training for battle.* "Praise be to the LORD my Rock, who trains my hands for war, my fingers for battle" (Ps. 144:1).

- *Walk moment-by-moment with the Spirit.* "Live freely, animated and motivated by God's Spirit. Then you won't feed the compulsions of selfishness . . . that is at odds with a free spirit" (Gal. 5:16–18 MSG). Ask yourself, in this moment, *Am I being led by my desires, ideas, or judgments—or by God's?*

- *Return to your standing as a royal daughter.* Consider all the things outstanding fathers do. Write a list of everything you can come up with. In so many ways, God is even better than this list. Return back to this often, when you start to feel you have to fight on your own.

- *See your war zone as God-owned territory (because it is).* God is your keeper.
- *Consider God using His heavenly forces on your behalf.* "The angel of the LORD encamps around those who fear him, and he delivers them" (Ps. 34:7).
- *Raise faith.* "Take up the shield of faith, with which you can extinguish all the flaming arrows of the evil one" (Eph. 6:16).

Second L: Jesus Is the Lamb of God

> Behold, *the Lamb of God*, who takes away the sin of the world! (John 1:29 ESV, emphasis added)

> And they overcame him because of the blood of the Lamb and because of the word of their testimony, and they did not love their life even when faced with death. (Rev. 12:11 NASB)

Jesus gave up His life, as the spotless Lamb. How can we live lamblike?

- *Choose to rest.* Because Jesus laid down His life, you can rest in His finished work. Imagine Jesus holding you.
- *Give your life away.* Give away the best of who you are, what you've learned, and what you own, because you're sure this is how Christ's love breaks out.
- *Lay your issues out on the table.* Give people a chance to know you. Give them a chance to uplift, encourage, and help you. Give them a chance to step out in ministry.
- *Affirm your wait* (consider all the reasons why it is valuable). Better things are still to come, but it is what God is doing in you today that helps you recognize and enjoy them when they finally do arrive.

- *Say thank you.* There are probably millions of unseen times that God has literally saved you from demise, accidents, and mayhem. Give thanks for what you cannot see. Also give thanks for what you can see.

- *Remember Jesus's sacrifice, His outpouring love.* "The blood of Jesus, his Son, purifies us from all sin" (1 John 1:7). Remember Jesus often. Love on Him.

- *Note the season.* Jesus knew there was a time to live, a time to teach, and a time to die. To know your season is to connect to what God is doing. Sufferers gain God's nearness. Celebrators find God's joyful heart. Mourners find God's presence. Tired ones find God's rest for their souls.

  Keep in step with your season. I've noticed that to step outside a season prematurely is to invite pain. It's the equivalent of wearing a bathing suit in a snowstorm and then blaming God for your frostbite. Embrace the season, with God, for what it is and He'll take care of you until spring arrives.

- *Get unconcerned with the stadiums.* You don't "perform" for others; you die for Jesus.

- *Embrace the cross.* "If anyone would come after me, let him deny himself and take up his cross and follow me" (Matt. 16:24 ESV).

- *Let God's grace lead you to love.* Abundant grace covers endless wrongs. Remind yourself of this often.

Third L: Jesus Is Love

God is *love*, and whoever abides in love abides in God, and God abides in him. (1 John 4:16 ESV)

If Jesus is Love, how do you stay in His love and love others?

- *Be.* Spend time with Him who is Love, to love.

- *Be curious.* Interestingly, someone mentioned to me that the opposite of fear is curiousness. To be curious is to fear less.

As you feel afraid to love others, invoke your curious side. Ask: *How might this make a person feel if I follow through with this love-act? How might I feel? What doors might God open through this?*

- *"Don't sweat the small stuff."* Let go of the small fights, small discouragements, small offenses . . . to offer big mercy, big hope, and big forgiveness.

- *Stop trying to be perfect.* If you seek after something that God never gave you, you'll always be discontent.

- *See potential.* Notice in others what they themselves can't see.

- *Notice your progress.* Acknowledge how you've changed, grown, and transformed. Incline your heart toward awe and wonder at the powerful working nature of God-in-you.

- *Ease up.* Love doesn't get far when it acts like a judge, dictator, or boss.

Lion walks out stripe-faced and ready to go. Lamb comes out clean and lays down His life. Love conquers all and never fails. But all three have one thing in common: an intensity that the ferocity of the enemy can't deal with.

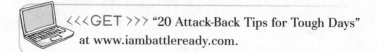 <<<GET >>> "20 Attack-Back Tips for Tough Days" at www.iambattleready.com.

DON'T *Fold*

GOD'S GIVEN YOU A

Good Hand

GUNSHOTS CAN EQUAL *Safety*

BE *Lion, Lamb,*

AND *Love*

A MIND TO CONQUER

*Intensity is what takes you from here to there
with full knowledge; you are going to arrive.*

PRAY

*God, will You magnify Christ in me? Will You pour out
grace on me that I might know, love, and look like You more
and more? You are my greatest gift, highest reward, and the
ultimate prize of my life. Help me not to get distracted by
lesser things when I have the best thing right before me, in
You. Thank You for Your love. Thank You for the good hand
You have given me. In Jesus's name I pray. Amen.*

WRITE THREE THINGS YOU'RE THANKFUL FOR

1. _____

2. _____

3. _____

ENTER YOUR MIND

Healthy striving is self-focused: "How can I improve?" Perfectionism is other-focused: "What will they think?"[2]

EXAMINE YOUR STORY

1. When do you most think you have a bad hand? And that another's is far better?

2. When do you compare, envy, or covet? How does that throw you off?

3. Write out all the ways in your life you've noticed (1) God really loves you; (2) you have conquered through Him (Rom. 8:37); (3) He gives you a door out of temptation (1 Cor. 10:13).

4. What is this chapter compelling you to let go of? To adopt?

EXPLORE WITH GROUP STUDY

1. What did you learn from your personal study time?

2. Regarding the enemy's five-pronged attack, what most gets you?

3. Which of the F.I.G.H.T.E.R. attributes trip you up in your day? Tell of a recent time you got held up.

4. God calls you holy, pure, and blameless in His sight. How does this change your hand?

5. Share stories of how prayer has worked in your life. How has faith worked?

6. What would it look like in your life to practically be lion, lamb, and love?

A CHRIST-CENTERED PRINCIPLE GOD BLESSES

On-fire intensity

Don't burn out; keep yourselves fueled and aflame. Be alert servants of the Master, cheerfully expectant. Don't quit in hard times; pray all the harder. (Rom. 12:11–13 MSG)

⋙···Warrior Mind-Set Twelve ····▸

*It's Not about What You Can or Can't Do,
It's Only about What He Can Do—through You*

(Impossibility)

"'If you can'?" said Jesus. "Everything is possible for one
who believes."

Mark 9:23

Point 1: Imagine If . . .

What if Moses thought his story ended after Pharaoh freed the
Israelites by saying, "Go, worship the LORD" (Exod. 10:24)? He
likely wouldn't have raised that mighty staff in such wild faith and
seen God part the Red Sea. And he probably would've missed a
chance to lay eyes on the promised land (Exod. 14; Num. 27:12).

What if Mary never sat down at Jesus's feet to listen? All us
women would think we have to go, go, go . . . strive, strive, strive
(Luke 10:38–42).

What if "the sinful woman" never poured out nearly a life saving's worth of perfume on Jesus because she didn't want to seem
"odd," "too much," "over the top," or "a show-off"? She'd never
have heard Jesus recognize her before man as He said, "You did

not give me a kiss, but this woman, from the time I entered, has not stopped kissing my feet. You did not put oil on my head, but she has poured perfume on my feet. Therefore, I tell you, her many sins have been forgiven—as her great love has shown. But whoever has been forgiven little loves little" (Luke 7:45–47).

What if Mary thought herself unworthy to anoint Jesus's body after His death, or simply not "as good as the men"? I wonder if she'd still have been the first to see Jesus risen. I also wonder if she would have been commissioned to share the story of His resurrection glory (see John 20:17).

These stories all have something in common. Do you see it? These people desperately believed in God more than their very good reasons not to.

Point 2: Lies! Lies! Lies! Five Lies We Need to Stop Believing

There will always be a very good, logical, and profound reason why we think God can't—or won't—do something. We're pros at rationalizing disbelief.

Our most popular doubts sound just like this:

1. I am not where I should be.

In response to this doubt, we pursue a self-improvement plan, PhD-level biblical knowledge, righteous acts, a show-offy spiritual life, or worse, we give up.

God "equip[s] his people to do every good work" (2 Tim. 3:17 NLT). "His divine power has given us everything we need for a godly life through our knowledge of him who called us by his own glory and goodness" (2 Pet. 1:3).

2. I need what I need—now.

Take any high-maintenance, I-want-it-now demands and boot them out the door of your life. You don't want to resemble the tantrum-throwing child on Christmas, the mega-smart and suicidal Wall Street investment banker, the lottery winner gone broke, or Satan. Sure, these people got what they wanted, but did it fill their heart?

Truly, what we want is Christ, to look like Him and to remain near Him. This is contentment.

Contentment says, "And God is able to bless [me] abundantly, so that in all things at all times, [I have] all [I] need, [and I] will abound in every good work" (2 Cor. 9:8). It expectantly reminds itself of what's to come by what's past: "I would have despaired unless I had believed that I would see the goodness of the Lord in the land of the living" (Ps. 27:13 NASB).

You hardly need more when you understand you have and are continuing to get *everything*.

3. I can't forgive myself for the past or for my present.

What person ever got better by constantly beating themselves up? Jesus took the beating so you don't have to. You don't have to go through months of self-hatred, weeks of constant pleading and crying, or the torture of self-inflicted distance from God.

When Jesus said, "It is finished," He meant it. When you say you're sorry and change your mind to go a new way, that is it. It is done.

"If we confess our sins, he is faithful and just and will forgive us our sins" (1 John 1:9). "As far as the east is from the west, so far has he removed our transgressions from us" (Ps. 103:12).

This means:

- God hears and accepts your apology.
- He forgives.
- He will faithfully help you chart a new course.
- You can stop hard-driving yourself to meet impossible expectations.

4. I trusted God, but He let me down. I can't trust Him again.

Did He really let you down? Fear says He did. But what does curiosity have to teach you as it pertains to this pain point?
Ask yourself:

- Is God still at work with this hurt?
- What might He be teaching me through it?
- How might He come through in a better way than I expected?
- What benefit might time lend?
- How might others have seen the glory of God shine through my moment of hardship?

I've come to find that God really has a heart for the greater good. Often it surpasses what our eyes can see.

5. I'm not who God says I am; I'm who I feel I am.

You are who He says you are. Even if you don't feel it, because your feelings lie. They're like passing winds. Follow them every direction and you'll go nowhere, bumping your head into glass doors. Rock-solid truth is Christ in you. I assure you, you 100 percent are who God says you are.

Point 3: Why It's Okay If You Feel You're Cracking along the Way

When we moved into our new home, I realized I had no plates. I'd donated them all before our move. Now we had nothing to eat on. The only plates left were ones stored in the garage. They were tightly packed with little tissues between each plate, all packaged up in a big plastic bin. After thirteen years, and twelve moves, astonishingly, they were hardly used.

I remembered the day I got that china. It was on my wedding day. I'd opened them a little, to look at their ornate perfection. And that was it. I hardly touched them again: I didn't want to chip their beauty, crack their edges, or destroy their fragility. So, year after year, I carted them around with me, city to city, safely boxed up.

Until now. Until getting here, to this last chapter of this book. Here, I see the horrific error in boxing up beauty meant to come out.

It is not safety but risk. It is a huge risk to box up God's best and to leave it collecting dust. Inaction is destruction of what God has created. It also silently says, "God is not able."

I am not blind. I am no longer deaf. Before me is a picture of what I am squandering.

Also before me is the truth: better are a million chips along the way than cobwebby, wasted beauty.

What beauty have you boxed up? What might God want to let out?

Note here the reasons why you've kept these things boxed up:

_____

_____

_____

_____

Write yourself words of encouragement as to why you can let out what you've kept in so long:

_____

_____

_____

_____

And consider these things as you build your list:

1. A woman can appear entirely successful by the world's standards and still feel utterly unused and internally bruised as she does so. Just because you are good at something, or people note you are, doesn't mean it is what you are meant to do.

2. God can make up for all the wasted years in a split-second.

3. God doesn't give bad gifts.

4. The God who *was*, is, and is to come (Rev. 1:8) is fully able to fix what needs fixing for your today. He can do all things.

5. Your gift will make room for you (Prov. 18:16). Even if you don't know how the world could need another *you*, when you're true to you, God will make room for you.

6. There is a reason you're alive. The world needs what God has given you to offer.

7. Every work is ultimately God's work. You just meet Him there and do it with Him.

8. If you have less fear and doubt, you'll get more wisdom and revelation.

9. It's not the public perception of anointing that makes you anointed. Great giftings largely unseen by people often are powerfully seen and utilized by God (think of the good Samaritan and David in his really early days).

10. Waits are good. The kettle needs time to boil. In your wait, take time to soak in the fire of God. At the proper time, the whistle will sound and God will use what He fired up in you.

Beyond every statement of doubt is an opportunity of new faith. We don't have to be angry that we doubted, we just have to be equipped with a comeback of truth. This is how we see through what tries to darken our day.

Point 4: Faith, Meet My Friend, _____

There is a new friend I'd like you to meet.

Faith, meet [insert your name here].
[Insert your name here], meet Faith.

From this point on, I want you to get to know each other well. Faith? The great thing about Faith is that she is your risk-taking friend. The one you're not always quite so sure you can trust—but do. Trust her. She always comes through. Don't worry about your gut instinct not to believe her.

She'll always be with you to help you along your way.

She doesn't let down or lead wrong, even when you can't immediately see an answer or even if it appears she's led you into a dark alley. By morning you'll say, "Oh, that's why you did it that way." Give her time. She does things God's way.

There's a good plan in motion.

She believes in what your flesh can't. She sees what your earthly eyes won't. She knows the way even if you've undoubtedly decided, *There's no way.* She's awesome.

To let her work looks like:

- Doing in humility what pride tries to negate.
- Knowing God is up to something, even during trials.
- Dwelling on the wisdom stored up through trials.
- Giving yourself a pep talk when life goes bad.
- Living adored by God.
- Extending your best to others.
- Just doing it anyway, even though . . . despite the fact . . . even when . . .
- Trusting God to change you.
- Letting God's Word come alive.
- Speaking life, encouragement, and hope, always.

- Loving continually.
- Saying yes to God when every emotion says no.

Faith, in you, feels tired, but she puts on her running shoes anyway. Then she keeps going. Running. Activating stuff. She doesn't stop.

Even when you say:

"I don't feel like it."

"I don't have it in me to do what God wants."

"I don't see any reason to believe this will happen."

"I'm incapable. My track record stinks."

"I don't have enough [support, encouragement, resources, strength]."

Faith doesn't care. She gets things done because she knows it is not up to her but up to God. Nothing can stop Him. God will prevail.

Faith has the middle name Hope. Love is her friend. Grace tags along. Together, these four are a powerhouse group.

They unlimit the will of Jesus Christ working in and through you.

So you truly believe in:

Healing: "'Go,' said Jesus, 'your faith has healed you'" (Mark 10:52).

Answers: "Therefore I tell you, whatever you ask for in prayer, believe that you have received it, and it will be yours" (Mark 11:24).

God: "Then Jesus said, 'Did I not tell you that if you believe, you will see the glory of God?'" (John 11:40).

Your salvation: "If you declare with your mouth, 'Jesus is Lord,' and believe in your heart that God raised him from the dead, you will be saved" (Rom. 10:9).

Your vision: "If you have faith as small as a mustard seed, you can say to this mountain, 'Move from here to there,' and it will move. Nothing will be impossible for you" (Matt. 17:20).

God's renewing strength: "But those who hope in the LORD will renew their strength" (Isa. 40:31).

Your ultimate direction: "Trust in the LORD with all your heart and lean not on your own understanding; in all your ways submit to him, and he will make your paths straight" (Prov. 3:5–6).

Restoration: "And the God of all grace, who called you to his eternal glory in Christ, after you have suffered a little while, will himself restore you and make you strong, firm and steadfast" (1 Pet. 5:10).

Faith takes you where your own nature never could. She is your godly vision. She gives sight to the unbelievable.

Point 5: Last Things Last

I must triple-remind you: what impossible things you don't write down, you likely won't do.

If you read this book with just a thought to (1) keep in touch with God on this soul-transformation process; (2) focus on "stuff"; (3) see things through . . . I lament, you likely won't tackle anything. I have seen this happen nearly a hundred times in my life.

Recently, after writing this book, I was hit by a vicious struggle—and I struggled. Why? Because I forgot my personal daily attack plan. I forgot "my fight." I forgot the things that flick me, that send me over the edge, and that set me off. I took for granted the knowledge I had and didn't pay attention to it. We want to avoid this.

Anyone can read two hundred and some pages of ideas, but not everyone can put those ideas to work in their life. We want all our time together to count. We want our thoughts to stand strong. We want to sow deep roots that reap strong faith that allows us to see God's great plans through.

Write It Down

Wisdom is addressing specific points of change with the intention to implement them at a specific time. Wisdom also uses statistics to its advantage. We actually have a 42 percent greater likelihood of reaching our goals if we write them down.[1] If we get specific, targeted, and time-lined, our goal moves from hazy, like a foggy window, to clear, like a super-high-definition screen.

Clarity becomes our progress. Vision sees us through. I want us both to succeed.

And we can. First take the quiz, "What's My Battle Style?" This will help you identify ways that you can fight. Also develop your daily battle plan to have a specific fight-back approach to what tries to get you down. Finally, consider using the Battle Ready Daily Prayer Journal to focus your day. These tools used in tandem will lead to progress and success.

Get these and other memory tools and faith-building resources at www.iambattleready.com.

May God

> fill you with the knowledge of his will through all the wisdom and understanding that the Spirit gives, so that you may live a life worthy of the Lord and please him in every way: bearing fruit in every good work, growing in the knowledge of God, being strengthened with all power according to his glorious might so that you may have great endurance and patience. (Col. 1:9–11)

Seize the Moment

Before we wrap up, I must tell you: seize the moment. If one phrase summarizes the whole book, this is it. Make a momentary decision to think right. You know how to do this now. So do it in the moment you have. Then keep doing it.

Moments make up your life. Think right in this moment, then the next, and the next, and you will be well on your way. A moment multiplied makes up a minute, then an hour, then a week . . . until sixty-six days of habit change are complete.

Life change is always done one moment at a time. Seize the moment. Sow there. Sift there. Filter there. Lion, Lamb, and Love there. Repeat. Three steps forward. One or two back. Giant leap!

Don't give up. Bounce back.

Let days heap on days and make some mistakes along the way, but stay with God and Faith. Let yourself marvel along the way. And remember: "This is what the LORD says to you: 'Do not be afraid or discouraged because of this vast army. For the battle is not yours, but God's'" (2 Chron. 20:15).

<<<DOWNLOAD >>> your Daily Battle Ready Plan or take the "What's My Battle Style" quiz at www.iambattleready.com.

WHAT IF YOU *Believed?*

❦

GOD *Forgives* INSTANTLY

❦

BETTER ARE CHIPS THAN
Wasted Beauty

❦

MEET *Faith*

❦

Seize THE MOMENT

A MIND TO CONQUER

Without faith, life sinks like dead weight.

PRAY

God, there are no limitations for You. There are no boundaries for Your love. There is no thing that is too great for You to do. I completely and unequivocally trust You. I give my life to You. I give my soul to You. I give my dreams to You. You are more than enough, and Your will is more than enough for me to rest on and trust in. In Jesus's name. Amen.

WRITE THREE THINGS YOU'RE THANKFUL FOR

1. _____

2. _____

3. _____

ENTER YOUR MIND

Neurology and spirituality researcher Dr. Andrew Newberg states,

With spiritual practices, the more you do it, the more you do it. That is, the more people can be encouraged to prayer, to engage their church and the people in it, to do charitable work, the more these concepts become a part of how your brain functions. With ongoing practice, you can do these things more easily and you want to do them more. You become "wired" for it. Whether meditation, prayer, reading the Bible, discussing the Bible, or Bible studies, they change your brain, making you more receptive. . . . The brain also benefits from your being optimistic and having faith. Enthusiasm is important, as well.[2]

Keep on filtering your thoughts; over time, this practice will change them.

EXAMINE YOUR STORY

1. Which of the five lies have you believed? What truth can you now seize?

2. What new, innovative things could you do, now that you are beginning to believe God can do anything through you? (Brainstorm all the possibilities.)

3. What will happen if you try to work this whole book by your own effort?

4. Why does grabbing hold of a momentary decision help you to move forward? What does it release you from?

EXPLORE WITH GROUP STUDY

1. How has God changed you and renewed you through this book?

2. What are you believing for? What lie has snagged you?

3. What grace do you need to take with you along the way?

4. What words from the mouth of your friend, Faith, do you need to remember?

5. What is the one quality of God that your heart most needs to cling to today? Why?

6. What might Christians look like if we all trained our mind and rose up and into our godly calling? How might our world change?

A CHRIST-CENTERED PRINCIPLE
GOD BLESSES

Impossibility that is more than possible with Jesus

God can do anything, you know—far more than you could ever imagine or guess or request in your wildest dreams! He does it not by pushing us around but by working within us, his Spirit deeply and gently within us. (Eph. 3:20 MSG)

Tying Up Loose Ends

If this book has caused even the smallest amount of breakthrough for you, I must hear about it! Let's celebrate together. Share your story on social media with me @kellybalarie using the hashtag #battlereadybook.

Be sure to visit www.iambattleready.com for mind tools, faith-building resources, and daily battle plan downloads.

If you are facing a battle that is hard, why not let the community of #battlereadybook sisters pray for you? Tweet, Facebook, or Instagram with #battlereadybook and we'll jump in, pray, and encourage you.

Acknowledgments

Thank You, God. I love You. I thank You. I know You are in these pages. That is what matters. Thank You for choosing me and using me to bless people. What an honor! Thank You also for placing around me people who love me and help me to see You—my husband Emanuel, our friends, our family, the Harbour church, and our two kids, Michael and Maddie (my cute-ifuls). Thank You for Amanda Luedeke, Jamie Chavez, and the Baker Books team; I'm astonished at how they so graciously go above and beyond for me every time. I thank you that this book will free women's minds; it will bring clarity and it will forge freedom in powerful ways. Jesus, You fought the greatest battle ever fought, You died, and then You won to reign in victory always and forevermore. Thank You for transformation. Thank You that we are day-by-day becoming bigger, better, and bolder love fighters who exalt Your name, who keep on fighting, and who don't give up.

Notes

Warrior Mind-Set One

1. "Memory Capacity of Brain Is 10 Times More Than Previously Thought," *Salk News*, January 20, 2016, http://www.salk.edu/news-release/memory-capacity-of-brain-is-10-times-more-than-previously-thought/.

2. Shad Helmstetter, *What to Say When You Talk to Yourself* (New York: Pocket Books, 1980), 66.

3. University of Chicago Press Journals, "Negativity Is Contagious, Study Finds," *ScienceDaily*, October 7, 2007, <www.sciencedaily.com/releases/2007/10/071004135757.htm>.

4. Rick Hanson, *Hardwiring Happiness: The New Brain Science of Contentment, Calm, and Confidence* (New York: Harmony, 2013), 13.

Warrior Mind-Set Two

1. Timothy Gallwey, *The Inner Game of Tennis: The Classic Guide to the Mental Side of Peak Performance* (New York: Random House, 1974, 1977).

2. Matthew Brown, "Father's Faith: Perceptions of God May Stem from Dad-Child Relationships," *Washington Times*, June 15, 2013, http://www.washingtontimes.com/news/2013/jun/15/fathers-faith-perceptions-god-may-stem-dad-child-r/FB0E12F73C5B0C718CDDAA0894.

3. Ashley Merryman, "What Do Children Understand about God?" *Newsweek*, August 29, 2009, http://www.newsweek.com/what-do-children-understand-about-god-223404.

Warrior Mind-Set Three

1. Some of these examples were gathered from John M. Grohol, "15 Common Defense Mechanisms," *PsychCentral*, accessed December 11, 2017, https://psychcentral.com/lib/15-common-defense-mechanisms/; Psychologist World, "31 Psychological Defense Mechanisms Explained," accessed December 11, 2017, https://www.psychologistworld.com/freud/defence-mechanisms-list.

2. HeartMath Institute, "The Heart-Brain Connection," accessed December 11, 2017, https://www.heartmath.org/programs/emwave-self-regulation-technology-theoretical-basis/.

3. Newsweek Staff, "Psychology: Why Some Don't Learn from Their Mistakes," *Newsweek*, April 23, 2007, http://www.newsweek.com/psychology-why-some-dont-learn-their-mistakes-97865.

Warrior Mind-Set Four

1. Katherine Rundell, "Confessions of an Amateur Tightrope Walker," *New York Times*, December 2, 2016, www.nytimes.com/2016/12/02/opinion/confessions-of-an-amateur-tightrope-walker.html.

2. James Clear, "How Long Does It Actually Take to Form a New Habit? (Backed by Science)," *James Clear*, accessed December 11, 2017, http://jamesclear.com/new-habit.

3. Hal Ersner-Hershfield, Tess Garton, Kacey Ballard, Gregory Samanez-Larkin, and Brian Knutson, "Don't Stop Thinking about Tomorrow: Individual Differences in Future Self-Continuity Account for Saving," *Political Perspectives* 29 (March 1990): 45–60.

4. Todd Rogers, Katherine L. Milkman, Leslie K. John, and Michael I. Norton, "Beyond Good Intentions: Prompting People to Make Plans Improves Follow-through on Important Tasks," *Behavioral Science & Policy* 1, no. 2 (December 2015): 33–41, http://scholar.harvard.edu/files/todd_rogers/files/beyond_good.pdf.

5. Vivian Giang, "Neuroscience Says These Five Rituals Will Help Your Brain Stay in Peak Condition," *Quartz Media*, March 1, 2016, https://qz.com/626482/neuroscience-says-these-five-rituals-will-help-your-brain-stay-young/.

Warrior Mind-Set Five

1. Items 1 through 4 above are sourced from David R. Hamilton, "The 5 Side Effects of Kindness," *David R. Hamilton PhD*, May 30, 2011, http://drdavidhamilton.com/the-5-side-effects-of-kindness/.

2. Ellen Hendriksen, "3 Toxic Thinking Habits That Feed Your Insecurity," *Quick and Dirty Tips*, May 12, 2017, http://www.quickanddirtytips.com/health-fitness/mental-health/3-toxic-thinking-habits-that-feed-your-insecurity?utm_source=sciam&utm_campaign=sciam.

Warrior Mind-Set Six

1. Melissa Chan, "Here's How Winning the Lottery Makes You Miserable," *Time*, January 12, 2016, http://time.com/4176128/powerball-jackpot-lottery-winners/.

2. Adrian Furnham, "The Curse of Perfectionism," *Psychology Today*, February 12, 2014, https://www.psychologytoday.com/blog/sideways-view/201402/the-curse-perfectionism.

3. Melanie Greenberg, "The 3 Most Common Causes of Insecurity and How to Beat Them," *Psychology Today*, December 6, 2015, https://www.psychologytoday.com/blog/the-mindful-self-express/201512/the-3-most-common-causes-insecurity-and-how-beat-them.

Warrior Mind-Set Seven

1. Melanie Greenberg, "8 Ways to Bounce Back After a Disappointment," *Psychology Today*, June 30, 2015, https://www.psychologytoday.com/blog/the-mindful-self-express/201506/8-ways-bounce-back-after-disappointment.

Warrior Mind-Set Eight

1. Michael Winnick, "Putting a Finger on Our Phone Obsession," *dscout*, June, 16, 2017, https://blog.dscout.com/mobile-touches.
2. Kate Torgovnick May, "Does Having Choice Make Us Happy? 6 Studies That Suggest It Doesn't Always," July 18, 2012, *TED Blog*, http://blog.ted.com/does-having-choice-make-us-happy-6-studies-that-suggest-it-doesnt-always/.
3. May, "Does Having Choice Make Us Happy?"
4. Adrian F. Ward, Kristen Duke, Ayelet Gneezy, and Maarten W. Bos, "Brain Drain: The Mere Presence of One's Own Smartphone Reduces Available Cognitive Capacity," *The University of Chicago Press Journals* 2, no. 2 (2017): 140–54, http://www.journals.uchicago.edu/doi/abs/10.1086/691462.
5. Chris McChesney, Sean Covey, and Jim Huling, *The 4 Disciplines of Execution: Achieving Your Wildly Important Goals* (New York: Free Press, 2012), 26.
6. Leo Widrich, "Why We Have Our Best Ideas in the Shower: The Science of Creativity," *Buffer Social*, February 28, 2013, https://blog.bufferapp.com/why-we-have-our-best-ideas-in-the-shower-the-science-of-creativity.
7. Roxanne Bauer, "This Is Why Work Will Always Fill Up Your Time," *World Economic Forum*, November 6, 2015, https://www.weforum.org/agenda/2015/11/this-is-why-work-will-always-fill-up-your-time/.

Warrior Mind-Set Nine

1. Tara Parker-Pope, "The Generous Marriage," *New York Times*, December 8, 2011, https://well.blogs.nytimes.com/2011/12/08/is-generosity-better-than-sex/.
2. UnitedHealth Group, "Doing Good Is Good for You: 2013 Health and Volunteering Study," accessed December 8, 2017, http://www.unitedhealthgroup.com/~/media/uhg/pdf/2013/unh-health-volunteering-study.ashx.
3. Jennifer L. Trew and Lynn E. Alden, "Kindness Reduces Avoidance Goals in Socially Anxious Individuals," *Springer Motivation and Emotion* 39, no. 6 (2015), https://rd.springer.com/article/10.1007/s11031-015-9499-5.
4. Random Acts of Kindness Foundation, "Science of Kindness," accessed December 8, 2017, http://downloads.randomactsofkindness.org/RAK_Media_Kit/RAK-Science-of-Kindness-FAQ.pdf.

Warrior Mind-Set Ten

1. Ben C. Fletcher, "What Your Clothes Are Telling You," *Psychology Today*, May 27, 2014, https://www.psychologytoday.com/blog/do-something-different/201405/what-your-clothes-are-telling-you.
2. Jules Montague, "The Mind-Altering Power of Doubt," *The Week*, April 25, 2017, http://theweek.com/articles/694262/mindaltering-power-doubt.
3. Hanson, *Hardwiring Happiness*, 20.

Warrior Mind-Set Eleven

1. Dr. Charles Stanley, "Making Decisions God's Way," *InTouch*, February 5, 2015, https://www.intouch.org/read/magazine/daily-devotions/making-decisions-gods-way.

2. Brené Brown, *The Gifts of Imperfection* (Center City, MN: Hazelden Publishing, 2010), n.p.

Warrior Mind-Set Twelve

1. Mary Morrissey, "The Power of Writing Down Your Goals and Dreams," *Huffington Post*, September 14, 2017, http://www.huffingtonpost.com/mary morrissey/the-power-of-writing-down_b_12002348.html.

2. Robert Crosby, "Faith and the Brain: An Interview with Dr. Andrew Newberg," *Christianity Today*, Summer 2014, http://www.christianitytoday.com/pastors /2014/summer/faith-and-brain.html.

About the Author

Kelly Balarie is an author and national speaker on a mission to encourage others not to give up. Through times of extreme testing, Kelly has discovered peace-bringing wisdom, truth, and techniques that help women live full-hearted, even when life feels downright empty. Kelly believes there is hope for every woman, every battle, and every circumstance. She shares this hope on her blog, www .purposefulfaith.com, and in many publications such as *Christian Post*, *Relevant*, *Crosswalk*, and *Today's Christian Woman*. Kelly's work has been featured on *The Today Show*, 700 Club Interactive, Moody Radio, and other television and radio broadcasts. When Kelly is not writing, she is chilling at the beach with her husband, a latte, and two kids who rightfully demand she build them awesome sandcastles.

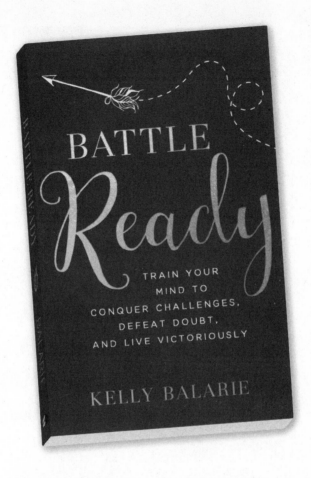

For a ton of *Battle Ready* bonuses and resources,
visit **iambattleready.com**

"Kelly shows us how we can overcome our greatest fears by developing the tenacious courage of a fear fighter who knows how to throw a strong faith punch!"

—Renee Swope, author of *A Confident Heart*

Take the 4 Days to Fearless Challenge
at **fearfightingbook.com**

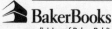

Connect with Kelly!

For more information and online resources, visit

PurposefulFaith.com

LIKE THIS BOOK?

Consider sharing it with others!

- Share or mention the book on your social media platforms. Use the hashtag **#BattleReadyBook**.

- Write a book review on your blog or on a retailer site.

- Pick up a copy for friends, family, or strangers— anyone who you think would enjoy and be challenged by its message.

- Share this message on Twitter or Facebook: **I loved #BattleReadyBook by @KellyBalarie // PurposefulFaith.com @ReadBakerBooks**

- Recommend this book for your church, workplace, book club, or class.

- Follow Baker Books on social media and tell us what you like.

 **Facebook.com/ReadBakerBooks**

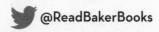 **@ReadBakerBooks**